THE GOD
WHO
GIVES IDEAS

By Roxanne Brant

Published by
ROXANNE BRANT MINISTRIES
NORTHERN FLORIDA CHRISTIAN CENTER, INC.
P. O. Box 1000
O'Brien, FL. 32071

Dedicated to:

REV. DIANE WALKER

with my best love.

Through her love and friendship,
my life has been enriched
and my ministry strengthened and increased.

Unless otherwise indicated, all Scripture quotations in this volume are from the *King James Version* of the Bible.

ISBN 0-915267-15-2
Printed in United States of America

TABLE OF CONTENTS

PREFACE

God delights in giving His children helpful, wonderful and inspiring ideas that will bless and prosper them. As we seek God's plan for our lives, living to please Him and serving others, He gives us marvelous ideas. When we follow each idea through to its conclusion, we find that problems are solved and that we are enjoying the fruitful lives that He has promised in His Word.

God gives us many kinds of ideas. However, the main focus of this book is that God gives us as Christians ideas that enable us to prosper materially so that we can be more effective channels of His blessings to others and help spread the gospel of Jesus Christ worldwide. He doesn't bless us so we can lay up treasures on earth.

This world is filled with greed and covetousness, and God wants us to be free from these harmful traits. He has told us to seek first His kingdom and righteousness (Matthew 6:33), giving Him first place in our lives. When we do, then He can trust us to properly handle the wealth He allows us to receive knowing we will use it to expand His kingdom and bring honor and glory to His name.

God's plan is that we will prosper "from the inside out"--spiritually, mentally and emotionally and then physically and financially (3 John 2). He intends for us to be *channels of distribution--not storehouses,* hoarding wealth. In God's plan, *riches are never to be pursued. Instead they are received as a blessing from God once our relationship with Him is right.*

The Bible tells us God financially blessed Abraham, Isaac, Jacob, Joseph, Joshua, David, Solomon, Job and many others. These men loved God. They put relationship with Him before riches, and God blessed them financially.

Material poverty is one of the curses that came about because of man's sin and separation from God in the Garden of Eden. However, the Bible tells us that Jesus became a curse for us. He took upon Himself not only our sins but also our diseases and our material poverty. He did this so we might receive God's grace in exchange: forgiveness of sin, eternal life, physical healing and material blessings (Galatians 3). Jesus Christ left the riches of Heaven and became poor so we might have a full supply of material things and be able to help others (2 Corinthians 8:9).

How can Christians who live in poverty and on food stamps build churches or construct and operate Christian television stations? How can they pay for mass media evangelism or send missionaries around the world to preach the good news of the gospel of Jesus Christ to the billions of people who still haven't heard it?

The devil has effectively indoctrinated many Christians with a "poverty complex." Jesus wants to free them from that bondage. They need to see that God has ideas He wants to give them that will greatly enrich them materially so their needs will be met. Then they can work with God in financing the preaching of the gospel throughout all nations of this world.

God is looking for people who want to help expand His kingdom on earth--not lay up riches for themselves! We serve God because we love Him and we help people because we love them. *WE DON'T SERVE GOD BECAUSE HE REWARDS US MATERIALLY OR OTHERWISE!* However, God has set up laws to govern this earth, such as the laws of sowing and reaping. This tells us GOD HAS A REWARD SYSTEM. He has told us to give out to help others and we will receive rewards in return. HOW WONDERFUL IT IS TO WORK WITH GOD.

The purpose of this book is to share insights that God has given me which will bless His people. This is by no means a complete study of the subject. This book was written to help you better understand some of God's laws

and equip you to be a more effective worker in His kingdom. I pray these truths will edify you and make you even
more fruitful in Jesus' service.

Roxanne Brant

CHAPTER 1

THE GOD WHO GIVES IDEAS

One small idea can change your life. One simple idea can turn you from material poverty to material prosperity almost overnight. An idea from God can bring you out of fear and despair into courage, confidence, faith and victory very simply.

God gives us all kinds of ideas. The Bible states (Genesis 1) that *God created the universe with words. He still rules it with His creative word!* God wants to drop His ideas into your mind every day much like a bird drops eggs into her nest. Many of the positive ideas that seem to "flow" into your mind are from God. Regretfully, our usual human tendency is to dismiss these ideas that come into our mind--ideas that, if pursued, would energize us, giving us a purpose and solutions to our problems.

GOD'S IDEAS ARE HIDDEN FOR US...NOT FROM US...IN CHRIST

Are you in a difficult situation? Do you find yourself entangled in "impossible circumstances" or problems? Problems, difficulties and "impossibilities" mean nothing if you are hooked up with God. *All you need to do is to accept the "higher ideas" of God to conquer these situations. God delights to supply ideas that will turn the impossible situations in your life to your good! He supplies the ideas. All you have to do is be open to receive them and then walk out these ideas in your daily living. God's ideas will always put you over into victory--all for His glory.*

Since God created this universe in all of its intricacy, balance and awesomeness, He knows how it all hangs together--how each portion operates and fits into the whole! He is not just a God of religious ideas, rather He is omniscient--has total knowledge--and greatly desires to supply the ideas that His children need in any area of life. He supplies mechanical ideas, scientific ideas, architectural ideas, ideas concerning our relationships with one another, and ideas in any other areas of life that we need.

The Bible tells us *in Christ are hidden all the treasures of wisdom and knowledge* (Colossians 2:3). This does not mean just spiritual knowledge. It means exactly what it says: ALL the wisdom and the knowledge we need to help us live out our lives in fruitful ways for God's glory, are hidden for us in Christ!

God delights to give us knowledge of "witty inventions" (Proverbs 8:12). He can drop an idea or invention into your mind that will help thousands or millions of people. God is the Solver of "impossible" problems, the One Who gives "breakthrough" ideas! He longs to increase your creative potential and release a tremendous flow of creative ideas and energy into your mind. These ideas will help you and bless others. His ideas, when followed through, will help you become a better person, one who glorifies Him, and you will be an inspiration to others. Our God is such a great God that He will turn even your mistakes into victory by giving you incredible ideas that are much higher than men's ideas.

God's ideas are higher and better than ours:

"For My thoughts are not your thoughts, neither are your ways My ways," saith the Lord.

"For as the heavens are higher than the earth, so are My ways higher than your ways, and My thoughts than your thoughts.

"For as the rain cometh down, and the snow from

*heaven, and returneth not thither, but watereth
the earth, and maketh it bring forth and bud,
that it may give seed to the sower, and bread to
the eater:*

*"So shall My word be that goeth forth out of My
mouth: it shall not return unto Me void, but it
shall accomplish that which I please, and it shall
prosper in the thing whereto I sent it."* (Isaiah
55:8-11)

GOD'S IDEAS ARE PRACTICAL, INCREDIBLE AND EXCITING!

God's ideas are practical, incredible and exciting! For
example, several years ago, a Christian lady dreamed that
she saw a magazine advertisement for beef stew which
included a freeze-dried sample of the stew right in the
middle of the advertisement. In her dream, this Christian
lady ripped open the sample, dropped it into a cup, poured
hot water over it and ate the stew. It was delicious.
Acting on her dream, she patented the idea for a small
investment. Time proved that this practical dream was from
God since she prospered, blessing her church with a financial gift. This enabled them to reach out more effectively
with the gospel of Jesus Christ. God cared enough about
practical things to give this Christian lady a truly practical
and innovative idea.

If you have asked Jesus Christ to become your Savior
and the Holy Spirit to dwell within you, God lives in you.
When He lives within you, His creative energy will flow
through your mind forming ideas that can change your circumstances, environment, business and future. These ideas
will gush up like living water.

Christians are in a position to receive God's ideas
easily when they get quiet before Him. He has made it
possible for us to receive communications (Colossians 1:12).
As we walk with God in an attitude of worship, He "flips
the divine switch" releasing an electrifying flow of His

9

ideas, knowledge and wisdom into our spirits. *These ideas come one at a time as needed.*

I know of a businessman who made soybean sauce before he became a Christian. His business took a turn for the worse and his company went bankrupt. Just when he was seriously contemplating suicide, someone told him about Jesus Christ. He asked Jesus to become his Savior and God began giving him one idea right after another. He told this businessman to buy a certain mountain so he got a real estate option on that mountain. People laughed at him but he placed a binder on the mountain and obtained a mortgage. Next God told him, "Call your new company Petros," meaning "rock" in Greek. Imagine the people's amazement when this Christian man discovered his mountain contained a vast quantity of a very valuable rock which was highly marketable in his part of the world! Orders for this extremely valuable rock came flooding in from businessmen all over that part of the world! Almost overnight, this man became a multimillionaire!

What did God do? *He just gave this businessman IDEAS.* The man received these ideas and walked them out as God instructed. God used these ideas to change this man's circumstances and greatly prosper him. Then this Christian businessman gave at least half of his material blessing to his church. He now feels "called" to the business world to make money to further the kingdom of God.

Another Christian businessman began to receive tremendous ideas after he became a Christian. God showed him, through an idea, how to make a *special adhesive chemical substance.* Since the construction industry is now using less nails and more adhesive chemicals, the idea was timely. This man patented the idea God gave him and is now selling his adhesive chemical substance worldwide. God gave him an idea, *showering down money upon him in the form of an idea.* That man is trusted by God and gives over half of his income for the propagation of the gospel.

Still another businessman gave his heart to the Lord and began to give God His tithe and liberal offerings. Then he began to receive a flow of ideas from God. He was shown how to change water, wood and certain chemicals into a product which acts like gasoline. This seems unbelievable; however, a patent lawyer watched as certain chemicals were drawn out of plants and trees, mixed with water and other chemicals. Then they put the mixture into his car and he drove it. The patent lawyer believes this product can partially solve a gasoline and oil shortgage. God gave the idea!

Sometimes God's children *"perish from lack of knowledge"* (Hosea 4:6). This is not God's fault for He is the God Who supplies ideas. He made this world and has ideas that will solve all of our difficulties and beautifully maintain the earth. All we have to do is simply receive His shower of ideas into our lives, give Him the credit and glory that He richly deserves, and then acknowledge His help by returning the material portion that He has commanded in His word.

FIVE BASIC WAYS TO RELEASE GOD'S IDEAS INTO YOUR LIFE

If you will consistently do these five things, you will tap God's revelation resources thereby releasing His ideas into your life:

1) Meditate on His Word.
2) Practice His Word.
3) Speak or vocalize His promises.
4) Pray. (This includes petition, praise and worship.)
5) Give materially to the work of God's church to advance His kingdom on earth.

We will discuss a little later how consistently practicing these five things will strengthen your ability to receive ideas, wisdom, knowledge and revelations from God.

11

FIVE PHASES IN THE DEVELOPMENT
OF AN IDEA

The idea that God "drops into your mind" can be incredible, life-giving and exciting. However, if you never plant or seriously consider it, like an unplanted seed, it will dry up or decay. An unhatched egg will rot in the nest. An idea must first be planted to bring forth fruit.

Often we edit or refuse the ideas that God drops into our minds. Later we see where another person has taken the same idea and turned it into a successful, fruitful venture. They obviously seriously considered the idea, felt it was worth trying, and reaped the benefit of following through on it.

FIRST, an idea must be planted or received.

SECOND, after you receive an idea, prove or test it. Is it Biblical? Will it fill a human need, solve a problem and help others?

THIRD, commit yourself to put that idea into action. Invest your time, money and energy and develop the idea.

FOURTH, know that problems or troubles will come in an attempt to stop or block you from completing the project. Trials always come before final victory. God will allow you to be tested and proved. When you are in this phase, you have to choose whether you will persist with your idea or vision or give up. Don't quit! Believe in the idea God has given you. Hang in there and you will eventually creatively and effectively move on to the final phase.

FIFTH, you will experience fulfillment and see fruit. Your dream will materialize, inspire and help others. After the storm is past, you will move into God's blessings.

Rev. Robert Schuller named these phases in a different way in Chapter 8 of his book entitled *"TOUGH TIMES NEVER LAST, BUT TOUGH PEOPLE DO."*

Rev. Schuller sees the following phases:

1) NESTING PHASE (You receive the idea from God.)
2) TESTING PHASE (Ask the right questions and see if the idea will meet human needs and inspire others.)
3) INVESTING PHASE (You commit your time, money and energy to the idea.)
4) ARRESTING PHASE (This is where problems and troubles will attack and try to block you. This is God's way of allowing you to be tested before the final victory.)
5) CRESTING PHASE (You scale the mountaintop and achieve success.)

Did you know that GOD'S "RICHES IN GLORY IN CHRIST" (Philippians 4:19) ARE NOT THINGS? The Holy Spirit showed me that THE RICHES IN GLORY IN CHRIST JESUS ARE IDEAS! God gives us these marvelous ideas to enrich our lives and make us fruitful, helpful and victorious so our lifestyles will inspire others. His ideas lead to victorious living, true prosperity and always glorify our Lord Jesus.

Recently while reading Philippians 4, I noted how the apostle Paul commended the early Christians for their delightful generosity in giving *once and again* to his ministry so he could preach Christ where His name was not known. Then inspired by the Holy Spirit, Paul gave this marvelous promise of God to them:

My God shall supply all your need according to (out of) His riches in glory in Christ Jesus. (Philippians 4:19)

Little did I know that God was about to reveal by His Spirit (through a series of illuminations and insights) a truth which would REVOLUTIONIZE my life and ministry. As I have shared this truth, many Christians have received it and moved from defeat into victory, from problems to prosperity, in different areas of their lives.

13

GOD IS YOUR SOURCE OF SUPPLY

When I researched the scripture, Philippians 4:19, I found the Holy Spirit, speaking through Paul, said, *"MY GOD shall supply all of your need...."* The pronoun is most emphatic here. Our Source of supply is God. He does and will provide for those who are faithful to Him.

Paul did not tell them, "The government or the labor unions will supply all of your need." He did not write, "Your employer, your retirement fund or the bank on the corner will supply all of your need." He simply stated, *"MY GOD will supply all of your need."* The Psalmist wrote, *"THE LORD is my shepherd; I shall not want"* (Psalm 23:1). If He is indeed our shepherd and God, why should we look to other sources for provisions? All of the natural sources are unreliable. They are merely conduits or delivery systems that God uses as He chooses.

God is a dependable supplier! In fact, *He is the only dependable supplier.* We are instructed to trust Him to supply all of our material needs--not institutions, people or certain situations. God is our only dependable Source of supply. He is wise, willing and able to abundantly supply, and will do so when we are open to receive, looking to HIM as our SOURCE.

When we speak of our needs, our speech should always show our trust in *Jehovah-Jireh,* "our provider," in *El Shaddai,* the God Who "abundantly pours forth" His goodness and provision into our lives.

How often, being human, we tend to lean on natural props. When this happens, God, in love, will usually permit our temporal supports to give way beneath us. Then we find ourselves flat on the ground, looking up, and saying, "I didn't realize that was a prop!" The cuts and scratches we acquire from such a fall should cause us to draw closer to our Father God as our only true and reliable Source of supply.

You may have heard someone say, "Well, God is a source, but that's just in the spiritual realm." Not true. God fashioned this entire earth and the surrounding universe with His hands. He created every natural resource that we find in or on this earth. Therefore, He is the God of this material world as well as the God of the supernatural world. It was God Who made man from the dust of the earth and placed him in the garden of Eden. God materially blessed Adam with every tree of the garden, giving him permission to freely partake of all of the trees with one exception--the tree of the knowledge of good and evil (Genesis 2:16,17).

God designed both the spiritual and physical worlds and He expects us to look to Him as our source of supply behind all of the varied "delivery systems" that He uses to convey His blessings into our lives. Since we are living in an era of tremendous economic upheaval, it is extremely important that we learn to trust God to supply all of our needs, both spiritually and materially, supernaturally and naturally. Many of us have had to learn this lesson over a period of years.

For example, Abraham maneuvered and connived in various ways, looking to human and material sources to bring about God's promise. It took him at least 40 years to begin to put his faith in God as his source of supply. God directed Abraham step by step and taught him to depend upon Himself. Abraham learned that when he put his total confidence (faith) in God, He would provide for him, keep him and prosper him in every area of his life.

It took at least 13 years before Joseph learned to depend upon God as his total source.

When Moses tried to rescue the Hebrew people in Egypt by his own power and strength, his efforts were a dismal failure. He had to flee the country to save his life. God sent him into the wilderness for a 40 year course in learning to trust Him and not rely on human resources. Finally, at the age of 80, Moses knew that God was the

15

only one he could depend upon to meet all of his needs--his total resource.

God patiently waits for each of us to totally surrender to Him and completely commit our lives into His keeping. *He wants us to trust Him completely and to realize that He is the only dependable source of supply behind all of the varied channels that He uses to bring blessings into our lives.* We need to wholeheartedly surrender ourselves to Him and know that even when we have impossible situations where it looks like we will "sink or swim, survive or perish," He will be there for us. When we are obedient to His word and walk in His wisdom, He will prosper us and receive glory as our lives become fruitful and we help others.

One of the first things God did for Abraham was to bless him materially. Abraham is called the father of faith. It is not wrong to be rich; it is how we use our riches that matters. God does not want us to amass riches for riches sake; rather He wants us to use them to advance His kingdom and bless others. The Bible does not say that "money" is the root of all evil. The Bible says that *"the LOVE OF MONEY is the root of all evil* (1 Timothy 6:10).

God does not want us to depend upon money as evidenced by His warning that *we are not to trust in uncertain riches* (1 Timothy 6:17). Jesus warned us about *"the deceitfulness of riches"* (Matthew 13:22). As we turn to God and trust Him to provide, He will give us wisdom, knowledge and all of the blessings of Heaven as well as add material things in a balanced way.

God's riches are inexhaustible and He knows our hearts. Once we begin to totally trust Him as our Source, He can begin to pour out the blessings we need knowing that His material blessings will not draw our attention away from Him as our only dependable Source.

THE MEASURE OF GOD'S SUPPLY

The measure of God's supply is infinite! There is an inexhaustible supply for each of our needs in the treasury of divine grace. There is a royal abundance, a wealth of blessings and unsearchable riches to be poured forth upon us from God. God is so good that He cannot be more good. We can add a drop of water to a massive ocean but we cannot add to the goodness of God. Out of His infinite and perfect goodness, God freely gives us good things in abundance to meet all of our needs.

Truly, as the apostle James wrote:

Every good and perfect gift is from above, and comes down from the Father of lights, with Whom is no variableness, neither shadow of turning. (James 1:17)

Because of His infinite goodness, our heavenly Father pours forth certain of His blessings not only on those who are good but even on evil and unjust people!

He maketh His sun to rise on the evil and on the good, and sendeth rain on the just and on the unjust. (Matthew 5:45)

God abundantly pours even more of His goodness and wealth of blessings into our lives when we meet the conditions He has set forth. We are then in a position to receive His marvelous, delightful blessings.

CONDITIONS TO BE MET BEFORE RECEIVING GOD'S SUPPLY

God has made provision for ALL of our needs to be met! This includes not only material necessities but also our spiritual, psychological and emotional needs. However, when I find a promise in the Bible, I always look for the CONDITIONS (or stipulations) that must be met so I will be in a position to receive God's promise.

The Philippians met three conditions which enabled Paul to give them the marvelous promise recorded in Philippians 4:19:

17

1) They were IN CHRIST--born again believers.
2) The Philippians were LIVING in accordance with the teachings of God's Word. (Remember Paul rejoiced because of their beautiful relationship with each other and the Lord as people who followed the truth of Jesus Christ.)
3) Not only were they living in accordance with God's Word, but they also met another condition: they were GIVING in accordance with God's Word. Paul said they gave *once and again to his necessity* (Philippians 4:16). More than any other church at that time, the Philippian church was faithful in supporting Paul's ministry. By giving to Paul, they gave into God's program for the expansion of His kingdom through the preaching of the gospel of Jesus Christ.

Paul wrote to the church at Philippi:

Now you Philippians know also that when I left Macedonia to begin ministering the gospel of Jesus Christ you are the only church that gave offerings to help me. Even in Thessalonica you sent time and again to relieve my need. Not because I desire a gift (money): but I desire fruit (interest) that may accumulate as a harvest of blessing to your account. (Philippians 4:15-17 paraphrased).

Then after receiving their most recent gift through Epaphroditus, Paul wrote:

But I have all, and abound: I am full, having received of Epaphroditus the things which were sent from you, an odor (fragrance) of a sweet smell, a sacrifice acceptable, well-pleasing to God. (Philippians 4:18)

The Philippians were givers. They gladly gave out of obedience and in love, as well as faith, according to the stipulations in God's Word. Their giving was acceptable and pleasing to God, much like a sweet-smelling fragrance.

We must fulfill the same conditions as the Philippians did if we want God's promise of supply to be effective for us:

1) We must be IN CHRIST--born again.
2) We must LIVE in accordance with the Word of God to the best of our ability.
3) We must GIVE our tithes and offerings to God according to His directions in the Scriptures.

If a person refuses to give tithes to God, you and I cannot promise them that God will meet all of their needs. They must first obey God's command to give if they want to receive the promised blessing.

God's Word tells us HE WILL SUPPLY ALL OF OUR NEEDS, and He means exactly that. He does not say that He MIGHT. Philippians 4:19 is a marvelous and delightfully exciting promise. It guarantees an ample supply of everything that we need! This verse is usually used with reference to materials needs. However, the Bible teaches us that God supplies not only our material needs, but also our spiritual, mental, emotional and physical needs as well. How wonderful it is to serve a God Who provides all that we need in such abundance!

Dear Reader,

Has God given you ideas that have prospered you? If so, would you share those experiences with us and give me permission to use your experiences as a source of encouragement for others? Of course, we will change names to avoid embarrassing someone.

Send your experiences to me and let us give God thanks for His marvelous ideas.

> *Roxanne Brant*
> *P. O. Box 1000*
> *O'Brien, FL. 32071*

Thank you. God bless you.

CHAPTER 2

THE HOLY SPIRIT BRINGS ILLUMINATION

As I read and studied the marvelous promise of Philippians 4:19, I realized that the phrase *"according to His riches in glory by Christ Jesus"* could be more accurately translated *"OUT OF His riches in glory"* or *"FROM His glorious resources in Christ Jesus."*

I wondered, "How does God provide for us?" *I wanted to understand HOW GOD OBTAINS WHAT WE NEED from His glorious resources in Christ. I also wanted to know, "What are His glorious resources in Christ Jesus?"*

Since this promise states that GOD SUPPLIES OUR NEEDS out of His glorious resources in Christ Jesus, I thought about needs. Our needs--not our desires--would be mostly material things. So let's say that we need food to eat. Also, before the end of the month, we will have to get four new tires for our car since the tread is gone on those we now have. We also owe a mortgage payment on our home and must get a new refrigerator. The old one leaks all over the floor!

Now we know that God doesn't rain groceries, car tires, mortgage payments, refrigerators and other things from Heaven to this earth. So I wondered, "What are His glorious resources in Christ Jesus?" I knew His Word says they are vast and inexhaustible and that He uses them to meet our needs. But I did not understand the connection between His riches or glorious resources in Christ and how they could be used to meet our needs. Since Christ Jesus is seated at the right hand of the Father in Heaven, I wondered, *"How does God get the material things that I need down here to me out of Christ Who is seated at His right hand?"*

The Bible tells us to ask and we will receive, so I asked God to reveal this truth to me in such a way that I could understand and teach it.   Soon the Holy Spirit gave me a whole new level of insight and illumination into this area of God's Word.   It has revolutionized my life and ministry.

I was impressed to read Luke, Chapter 16.   As I did, the Holy Spirit began to speak to me very clearly, giving me a *tremendous key* to unlock the meaning of Philippians 4:19.

GOD USES A KEY: LUKE 16:11

In Luke 16, verses 1-8, Jesus told a story about an unjust steward who laid up treasures for himself in dishonest ways.   Though rich in the things of this world, he was not rich toward God.   Jesus taught that people who take no thought for eternal things--but amass material possessions only for themselves--are foolish.   (See the parable of the rich fool in Luke 12:13-21.) Jesus said:

> *Take heed, and beware of covetousness (greed):*
> *for a man's life consists not in the abundance of*
> *the things which he possesses.* (Luke 12:15)

Our Lord taught that riches are perishable and cannot be relied upon to bring us happiness.   However, He also said that we can "make to ourselves friends of the mammon (riches) of unrighteousness." Then we can use these riches to help others and give toward the preaching of the gospel of Jesus Christ throughout the earth.   As a result, many will receive eternal life and enter Heaven.   We should primarily use our money to extend the preaching of the gospel and the kingdom of God on this earth.   The apostle Paul wrote Timothy:

> Instruct those who are rich in this life that they
> should not be proud or trust in uncertain riches,
> but they should rather trust in the living God Who
> richly gives us all things to enjoy. Tell them to
> use their money to do good, to be rich in good
> deeds, to practice sharing. By so doing, they
> will lay up riches for themselves that will endure
> in the life to come and lay hold on eternal life.
> (1 Timothy 6:17-19 paraphrased)

Jesus taught that money should be used to promote the kingdom of God and to help people. I read His comments after the parable of the dishonest steward in Luke 16:

> He that is faithful in that which is least is
> faithful also in much: and he that is unjust in the
> least is unjust also in much. (Luke 16:10)

This verse can be interpreted several ways. One is that a person who is faithful with seemingly little jobs or things, or small amounts of money, will also be faithful with more responsible work or things and large sums of money. Both the church and the business world have found this to be true. People start at the bottom of the corporate ladder and work their way to the top. No reputable corporation would think of putting an unproven person at the head of their company as president or chairman of the board. Instead corporate leaders keep close watch of their employees to make certain they are both capable and honest before they will promote them to a responsible position. Promotion is made only after the employee has proven to their satisfaction that he or she is faithful, honest, capable and will represent the company well.

However, I believe that this is the secondary and not the primary meaning of Luke 16:10. I believe verse 11 illuminates verse 10, as we shall see later. As I read verse 11, the Holy Spirit came all over me like warm oil and my heart began to pound. I knew I was supposed to pay close attention to verse 11. It reads:

23

If therefore you have not been faithful in the unrighteous mammon, who will commit to your trust the true riches? (Luke 16:11)

Unrighteous mammon is the wealth of this world. It is called "unrighteous" because much of it has been obtained dishonestly or used in covetous ways. True riches are not material. They are the heavenly, spiritual riches of God.

Jesus was saying:

So if you have proved untrustworthy in matters of the deceitful riches of this world, how can God trust you with the true riches of Heaven? (Luke 16:11 paraphrased)

Jesus said, "READ IT AGAIN." So I read verse 11 several times. I realized the meaning of this verse is basically that God cannot trust us with His ideas and revelations until we obediently respond to His command to give Him our tithes and offerings.

RELEASE MATERIAL GIFTS TO GOD AND RECEIVE IN RETURN HEAVEN'S RICHES AND REVELATIONS

Jesus told me, "Releasing material gifts for the use of God's kingdom and receiving the riches--wisdom, knowledge and revelations--of Heaven are connected." I was astounded! I had never seen this before:

RELEASE MATERIAL GIFTS FOR GOD'S WORK AND RECEIVE THE REVELATIONS AND BLESSINGS FROM HEAVEN (true riches) THAT YOU NEED!

The strobe light of the Holy Spirit so illuminated this verse that my heart beat rapidly. The words, *"Release Materially...Receive God's Revelations"* kept going over and over in my mind. "Read My statement in verse 11 in a POSITIVE way," Jesus said.

24

Looking again at the verse, I noticed that it appeared negative as written: *"If you have not been faithful."* So I reversed the order, placing the positive first, and did no injustice to the meaning: *"If therefore you have been faithful in the unrighteous mammon (material giving to God), then GOD WILL COMMIT TO YOUR TRUST THE TRUE RICHES."*

What a delightful, secure promise! When we release our material gifts, tithes and offerings, to the work of the kingdom of God, then Heaven's blessings and revelations are released into our lives.

As we release things in the material realm to God, He releases ideas, knowledge and wisdom for our everyday living from the supernatural realm in Heaven. These ideas will enable us to be victorious overcomers and bear much fruit to the glory of God here on earth.

I saw that the reference to *"that which is least"* in verse 10 meant money or material things. *"That which is much"* refers not to material things but to God's wisdom, ideas and heavenly blessings.

Therefore, if we are faithful in the least, giving our material gifts to God as He has prescribed in His Word, we will also be faithful in much. We will be faithful in receiving, transmitting and obediently walking in God's revelations and ideas. If we are not trustworthy in that which belongs to someone else, (God's material riches), then we cannot receive spiritual blessings and ideas from God.

I was amazed at how clearly God showed me that our releasing or giving of material gifts and our receiving revelations from Him are connected. THIS MEANS THAT THE FAITHFUL GIVER WILL RECEIVE MUCH REVELATION FROM GOD! I was so overcome with this powerful revelation that I began to pray in the spirit and worship God. He revealed that I was to read again Philippians 4:15-19. So I did. I knew even as I read this passage that the Holy Spirit was going to show me still more powerful truths.

THE HOLY SPIRIT SPEAKS

As I read Philippians 4:15-19 again, the Holy Spirit began to talk to me. First He asked, "WHO IS JESUS?" Now Jesus has at least 100 different names in the Scriptures, but I knew which name He wanted, so I replied, "JESUS IS THE WORD."

Then the Holy Spirit emphasized that ALL the treasures of wisdom and knowledge are hidden in Christ for us:

In Whom (Christ, the Word) are hid all the treasures of wisdom and knowledge." (Colossians 2:3)

It is important to understand that ALL wisdom and knowledge, both NATURAL and SPIRITUAL, are hidden in Christ. Knowledge, for example, of business and psychology, scientific knowledge and wisdom in medicine, geology, physics (as well as sales and management knowledge, etc.) is all hidden in Christ. The secrets for the cure for cancer are hidden in Christ. Hidden, NOT FROM US, but FOR US in Him!

This verse had thrilled me before, but I knew this was just another step toward what the Holy Spirit was going to show me. So I was not surprised when He told me, *"The Philippians GAVE ONCE AND AGAIN to Paul's ministry."* (See Philippians 4:16.)

I wondered, "What is He going to put together?" Then He said, *"According to Luke 16:11, the giving of material goods and subsequent release of revelations (riches) from Heaven are connected."* I agreed, "Yes, Holy Spirit, that makes sense."

Then He asked me, "If the Philippians gave materially unto Paul's necessity (to meet his material needs), what should they receive from God's treasury in Heaven?"

Suddenly, the answer exploded in my mind..."GOD'S IDEAS!" I saw clearly that God's riches in glory in Christ Jesus which Paul promised the Philippian Christians were NOT THINGS BUT REVELATIONS. In other words, Paul told them that God would abundantly bless them with ideas, wisdom, knowledge and revelation from His throne in Heaven through Christ Jesus, the Word.

I seemed to see, vividly, Paul standing before those faithful giving Philippian Christians saying, "I promise all of you who have given so faithfully that the GOD Whom I represent WILL SUPPLY EVERY NEED YOU HAVE OUT OF HIS GLORIOUS RESOURCES IN CHRIST JESUS."

The Philippian believers GIVING had tapped the eternal resources of God. Their giving loosed God's heavenly ideas, wisdom, knowledge and revelation into their lives to meet their needs.

I saw clearly that *God's riches in glory, or glorious resources, were not a rain of material things* such as refrigerators, food, mortgage payments or car tires pouring down from Heaven into our lives. *God's riches in glory in Christ are ideas which come to us to help us and prosper us.* As we walk in them, they lead us into prosperity and victory.

GOD'S PRINCIPLE OF RELEASING IN ORDER TO RECEIVE

When God was dealing with me about His principle of releasing to receive, I asked Him, "How can I effectively communicate what you have told me so that anyone can quickly understand this?" I truly wondered how people would respond when I told them, "Release your money into God's work and He will give you ideas that will cause you to prosper and inspire others as well."

God seemed to say, "Roxanne, this will not be hard for people to understand. Everyone who faithfully works for someone, giving their employer the benefit of their time,

27

knowledge, wisdom and ability (or ideas), expects their employer to pay them (by cash or check) as scheduled. The employee invests (or releases) his or her human wisdom, knowledge, ideas and flow of energy to benefit the employer. In turn, the employer gives the employee material substance or money. So there is a familiar exchange or connection between money and ideas in the business world today."

I appreciated His simple explanation that relates so well to things we are familiar with in our world. It is true that we do invest our knowledge, wisdom and ideas in this world to receive money. *However, since God is all wise, He does not need our ideas! Instead He tells us to give Him a tithe of our income and offerings as He instructs. Then God gives us wisdom, knowledge and ideas far beyond any worldly wisdom, knowledge or ideas that we could ever imagine.* What an exciting exchange! As we walk in the wisdom, knowledge and ideas that God gives us, we become more fruitful in all areas of our lives and God gets the glory.

Regretfully, many people faithfully give God their tithes and offerings and fail to realize He has something He wants to give them in return. So they go through life "barely making it!"

God has tremendous ideas and marvelous plans for our good. If we refuse to receive them, we can be compared to a person who goes to a soft drink machine, puts in his coins, presses the selection button and then immediately walks off without waiting for the drink to come down. The drink comes down, but he does not receive the benefit of it.

We would laugh at anyone who did something so foolish, but how many people do much the same thing spiritually? They give to God, "press the button" (their faith), and then go about their everyday activities totally oblivious to the fact that God has something He wants to give them. They don't take time to listen to God and see what He wants to communicate to them. Their actions indicate they don't expect anything from God.

28

God has tremendous ideas He wants to put in our spirits. We should always live with an attitude of expectancy, an anticipation that God is going to reveal something super, and patiently wait to receive His marvelous ideas!

When we give to God's work, He wants us to expect something from Him in return. His Word tells us, *"Give and it shall be given unto you."* *If we don't EXPECT TO RECEIVE, we won't be in a position to receive what He has for us.* For example, when a quarterback football player is preparing to pass the ball, his teammates should be alert to see where he is going to throw it. The player who fails to anticipate the ball coming his way may be caught "off guard," get hit in the head and fumble it. He certainly won't catch it!

The law of releasing to receive operates in different areas of life. For instance, when we forgive--release from personal judgment--a person who has hurt us, God releases us from His judgment. Then we receive God's forgiveness. God tells us to release first here on earth and then Heaven will release us. Jesus spoke about this several times:

> *For if you forgive others the wrongs they do to*
> *you, your heavenly Father will also forgive you:*
> *but if you don't forgive others their trespasses,*
> *neither will your Father forgive your trespasses.*
> (Matthew 6:14,15 paraphrased)

Jesus clearly told us that we must first release or forgive others before God will forgive us our trespasses, sins or wrong attitudes. There are numerous areas in our spiritual walk where we must first release something to God before God will release something from Heaven.

This is true in the area of material gifts. We are told to GIVE or release TO GOD FIRST and then God will abundantly release His wisdom, knowledge and ideas to us. Luke 16:10-12 clearly emphasizes this truth. If we faithfully give God His portion, God will give us true spiritual riches. The opposite is likewise true. If we WITHHOLD FROM GOD,

29

HE WILL WITHHOLD HIS SPIRITUAL BLESSINGS because we are not fulfilling our part of His spiritual law!

After seeing God's principle of releasing materially to receive God's revelations, ideas and blessings, I perceived more clearly that there were three basic ways of receiving material benefits from God.

AFTER GIVING, THERE ARE THREE BASIC WAYS TO RECEIVE FROM GOD.

The law of sowing and reaping with God's blessing of multiplication permeates all giving and receiving in God's kingdom.

1) As we give out materially to God, the Bible says that GOD WILL GIVE BACK TO US THROUGH PEOPLE. He will give us MONEY, THINGS THAT WE NEED, or WORK (which brings us the money we need).

Jesus said, *"Give and it shall be given unto you; good measure, pressed down, and shaken together, and running over, shall men give into your bosom. For with the same measure that you mete withal it shall be measured to you again."* (Luke 6:38)

Jesus clearly taught that the measure we use when we give something to others is the same measure others will use when they give to us. If we are a generous giver, others will be generous with us. The opposite is likewise true. If we are reluctant givers, tightfisted with our gifts, then others will repay us in kind.

God often gives to us through people that He uses as channels of His blessings. He frequently prompts people to offer someone a job so they will have the necessary income to provide for themselves. As we give to His kingdom work, God draws people to bring us more business, thereby increasing our income, so we can give out even more!

2) Sometimes instead of giving us new things through people, GOD just BLESSES WHAT WE ALREADY HAVE IN AN AMAZING WAY, saving us hundreds or thousands of dollars. He makes our equipment or car hold up longer. The Scriptures tell us God provided everything the Israelites needed during their wilderness journey. Their clothing and shoes lasted forty years! He is God of the present, as well as the past, and has been known to multiply food when needed. He even makes the desert "blossom as a rose." As you give out materially to His work, God may take your spindly fruit tree and make it bear 100-fold. He may make your used car function like a brand new one and give you twice as much service, saving you thousands of dollars. God delights to bless us and keep us and our families healthy.

3) Other times, GOD GIVES US IDEAS INSTEAD OF THINGS. When we walk in those ideas, they cause us to prosper materially and be fruitful. When our lives are fruitful, God is glorified. God's plan is that we will prosper from the inside out: spirit to soul to body to material circumstances! This glorifies God and will bring about the spreading of the gospel to the ends of the earth. Praise the Lord!

God is a generous giver. *He rains money upon us in the form of His creative ideas.* When we follow His ideas, they will transform our lifestyles, change our circumstances and relationships, and resolve business problems. There are no impossible situations where God is concerned. Impossible is not part of God's vocabulary!

As He talked to me, I was amazed at the series of vivid illustrations God gave me from my life, proving beyond doubt that *this principle will liberate millions of Christians worldwide IF they will follow His ideas daily.* When ALL of us who claim the name of Jesus practice this teaching, it will help millions of people, send the good news of Jesus to the ends of the earth and bring glory to our mighty God as He expands His kingdom.

As I mentioned previously, God showed me the principle in Luke 16:11 that when we release materially to Him, He responds by releasing His revelations and ideas (Heaven's "true riches") to us. That principle has revolutionized my life and ministry, but I need to explain further several aspects of it.

Dear Reader,

Has God given you ideas that have prospered you? If so, would you share those experiences with us and give me permission to use your experiences as a source of encouragement for others? Of course, we will change names to avoid embarrassing someone.

Send your experiences to me and let us give God thanks for His marvelous ideas.

> *Roxanne Brant*
> *P. O. Box 1000*
> *O'Brien, FL. 32071*

Thank you. God bless you.

CHAPTER 3

RELEASING GOD'S IDEAS TO MEET OUR EARTHLY NEEDS

As we said before, one of the ways we tap God's resources in glory in Christ Jesus is by giving material gifts to the work of God. He then releases heavenly ideas, wisdom, knowledge and revelations that will cause us to prosper.

In one of his sermons, Dr. Paul Yonggi Cho gave an example of this principle of giving to receive. One of his church members was taken home to Heaven and left behind him a middle-aged wife and three sons.

The widow made an appointment with Dr. Cho to obtain counseling. She said, "Pastor, my husband has died and left me $100,000, but we have three boys: one is going to the university, another is in high school and the youngest is in junior high school. I need to educate them all and I have not learned the ways of the business world. All three of my sons want to go to medical school. I will need at least $200,000 just for their education. How can I do this when I have only $100,000?"

Dr. Cho knew this was a very important concern of hers. So he wisely responded, "You need to recognize God as your total resource now. You need His help. God can help you even more than your late husband did."

This widow went home and prayed about the situation. She shared later that the Lord seemed to say to her, "You give one-tenth of the $100,000 your husband left you to My work, and I will bless the nine-tenths and take care of you and your sons."

Soon after the counseling session, she returned to Dr. Cho's office. With trembling hands, she laid an envelope containing $10,000 on his desk. She told Dr. Cho, "I give my tenth to the Lord in obedience and take Him as my source of supply." Both of them laid hands on the envelope and prayed turning her situation over to God. She left his office rejoicing that God had His portion and was going to provide for her family.

Several weeks passed. One day she returned to his office and said, "Dr. Cho, while I was praying, God gave me an idea. He told me I should invest the rest of my money ($90,000) in a certain piece of land in the northwest section of Seoul. This land looks much like wasteland. All of my friends think I'm foolish and that I will lose all of my money. But having peace in my heart, I have bought that piece of land."

During the next year, she continued to struggle and pray. All this time, God was working in her behalf "behind the scenes." God knows ALL things. So He knew what the future use of that land would be.

Time passed. One day, about a year later, the city government decided they needed the "wasteland" this widow had purchased for $90,000. They were planning big building projects near the land that this widow had bought and wanted to expand the transportation system to cover the increased number of people who would be moving into the area.

The leaders approached the widow with an offer. They told her they wanted to build a main subway station on her land. Their studies and population flow charts indicated her land was the "perfect place" for a desperately needed new subway station. They offered her a marvelous price!

She sold them the land for $290,000. After all of her expenses were taken out, including the taxes, she realized a net profit of $200,000 in one year's time! Were her friends amazed? Most certainly!

This little widow quickly wrote a check for $20,000 tithe and joyfully brought it to Dr. Cho saying, "God is wonderful. He has marvelously met all of our needs. In fact, God is treating me and my children even better than my late husband did!"

What did this Christian widow do? She simply gave her tithe as God told her to do. God, in turn, out of His glorious wealth in Jesus Christ, gave her an idea that prospered her. In a short period of time, that idea took her from financial need to tremendous prosperity. Her giving tapped God's resources. Because she gave, the kingdom of God was extended, the saints were blessed and missionary work was increased. Many people praised God, others came to know Jesus and received eternal life, and God was glorified!

This lady received only one idea, but it was certainly sufficient to take care of her and her sons! God abundantly met her need out of His riches in glory in Christ Jesus. This one idea, heavenly wisdom and knowledge, that the Holy Spirit gave her greatly prospered her.

When you need something from God, remember that if you want to benefit from the promise recorded in Philippians 4:19, you must first give materially to God. Then you can expect Him to bless you with the idea(s) you need. Just like a farmer, we must first "plant a seed" before we can expect a harvest. When we keep on giving to God, we should expect with great anticipation an abundant harvest of ideas.

ACCESS TO GOD'S IDEAS

Just as a child born into this world is an heir of their parents, so are we heirs of God when we receive Jesus as

Savior and are born into the family of God. One of the blessings or "birth rights" we receive as a child of God is that *we now have access to God's ideas,* wisdom, knowledge and revelation for the practical day-to-day living of this life.

At the point of new birth, God makes us capable of receiving His revelation and illumination. He gives us spiritual understanding and practical ideas that will move us into victory in all areas of our life. God's ideas make a difference right where the "rubber hits the road."

Paul told the Christians at Colossae that they should *give thanks unto the Father Who made them able (fit or qualified) to be partakers of the inheritance of the saints in light* (Colossians 1:12). In other words, the Bible teaches us that God has made it possible for you to receive His revelation as you walk in His kingdom of light, the kingdom of His Son Jesus Christ. (See 2 Corinthians 4:1-6.) God sends His ideas in many different ways to believers of all ages in all walks of life: government leaders, teachers, scientists, psychologists, businessmen, mechanics, housewives, students, and others.

As long as we keep releasing material gifts into the work of His kingdom, God will keep "throwing the divine switch" that releases an electrifying flow of His wisdom, knowledge and ideas into our spirits. These ideas come one at a time as needed.

How wonderful it is to know that when problems come in like a flood, as God's children, we can turn to our heavenly Father and obtain the wisdom we need to solve every problem. The Holy Spirit imparts ideas into our spirits. When we act on His ideas, we will always be victorious over every problem that comes our way. As we follow His ideas, He will even turn our mistakes into victories!

Sometimes, God gives us an idea which brings money our way. But other times God gives us an idea which saves us money, as in the case of some sick cattle we had several years ago.

GOD GIVES US A $1,000 IDEA!

We have a retreat center in Northern Florida. Several years ago, we decided that instead of mowing about sixty acres of grass we would purchase some cattle and let them be our "mobile mowing system." They would eat the grass and fertilize it as they moved about the grounds. We knew their "mowing" wouldn't produce the "smoothest" lawn around, but they would take the place of expensive equipment, gasoline and save us "muscle power" keeping the grounds neat.

Since we knew nothing about raising beef, our maintenance supervisor contacted a local veterinarian and obtained information about shots, feed and minerals that cattle would need. Then we purchased some cows in the spring of the year.

God blessed our herd of four-legged "lawn mowers" and things seemed to go smoothly that summer and fall. Then winter came. Because of our limited knowledge of cattle, we were not aware that they should be given a different diet in the wintertime if we wanted to have healthy cows. So we did not change their feed.

That winter, Carl, a retired cattle rancher and member of our board, came to visit us at our retreat center. He took one look at our cows and told us they were very sick, that they had numerous diseases due to malnutrition. Carl told me they were so far gone that they wouldn't respond to medical treatment. He said we should sell them right away and buy healthy cows, estimating that we would lose about $1,000 in the trade.

Carl told me he would be gone for six weeks, but then he would come back to the retreat center to check on the new cows for us. As I thanked him for his advice, he said, "REMEMBER, ROXANNE, YOU NEED TO GET THOSE

37

SICK CATTLE TO THE LIVESTOCK MARKET WHILE THEY ARE STILL STANDING UP!"

I thanked him for his help, waved good-by and went inside to talk with the Lord about the matter. I said, "Lord, I am sorry I didn't pray about the cattle. I know if I had been open to hear from You in this area, You would have shown me both the problem and the solution. I made a mistake. It is my fault. Please forgive me."

Instantly, I heard the Lord clearly say, "Roxanne, did I tell you to take the cattle to the livestock market?"

"No, Lord, Carl did." I answered.

"Roxanne, anoint the cattle with oil and I will heal them," Jesus said.

His instructions were so simple that I was absolutely astounded.

Jesus continued, "Roxanne, I can heal cattle easier than I can heal people because cattle don't have theology to overcome."

Naturally, I was excited. I immediately sent for our maintenance supervisor and told him all that the Lord had said. He was elated and went to find several bottles of cooking oil. We poured the oil into a pot and prayed over it, asking Jesus to fill it with His healing power so that the cattle would be healed when we anointed them.

Then I sat on the corral fence, near the gate, so I could easily anoint the cattle as he herded them past me one by one. I anointed every cow in the name of Jesus, placing a handful of oil on every one of them wherever I could. They literally rushed past me! I guess the sensation of oil dropping on them startled them. It was surely the fastest anointing service I have ever held and, without a doubt, the messiest one! However, they were all anointed...somewhere between their head and tail!

We had obeyed the Lord so we trusted His promise and believed they were healed. Six weeks later, Carl returned to the Center. Since he had told us to sell the cows, I wanted him to see them without knowing they were the same ones, and to get his reaction to what God had done. So I took him to see our cattle but did not tell him what we had done.

When Carl saw our cattle, he thought we had taken his advice and bought others. He said, "Roxanne, those are healthy, good looking cattle. How much did you lose in the swap?"

Deciding to have a little fun, I quickly added up the cost of the two bottles of oil and replied, "About $10.00." He stared at me--puzzled. Then I told him about the $1,000 idea God had given me. Carl, our cattle expert friend, praised the Lord and I began to comprehend what a great miracle the Lord had performed for us.

Through this experience, I learned that God wants us to come to Him all of the time for whatever we need, to recognize Him as our only totally dependable Source. We may be "experts" in certain areas of life, but if we will continue to seek and follow His leadings in our material giving and ask Him for His ideas *first* in every situation, then we will find our lives are far more productive and profitable.

DON'T EDIT GOD'S IDEAS.

We must take time to ask God for His ideas and then follow His instructions. If we don't, then we miss His ideas which are intended to help and bless us. Also, we should never "edit" God's ideas! In other words, when we first receive an idea, if we feel it isn't rational or sensible, *we shouldn't push it aside or try to improve on it*. If we do, we will be the poorer for it because God's ways are far superior to ours and His knowledge is perfect. Remember the Scripture says:

Trust in the Lord with all thine heart; and lean not unto thine own understanding.

In all thy ways acknowledge Him, and He shall direct thy paths. (Proverbs 3:5,6)

"...My thoughts are not your thoughts, neither are your ways My ways," saith the Lord.

"For as the heavens are higher than the earth, so are My ways higher than your ways, and My thoughts than your thoughts.

"...My word... shall not return unto Me void, but it shall accomplish that which I please, and it shall prosper in the thing whereto I sent it." (Isaiah 55:8,9,11)

God's ideas are exciting, creative and glorify Him! If you haven't tried them in every area of your life, try them. You'll be amazed at the results as you follow them.

When we read the Bible, we can see where many of the ideas, knowledge and wisdom that God gave to His leaders and people, both in the Old and New Testaments, seemed anything but wise or promising when He first gave it.

For instance, would you throw salt into a spring of water and then tell the people standing by you, "You can drink now. God says the water is pure."? That is basically what Elisha did according to the account in 2 Kings 2:19-22. The waters of Jericho were bad. Because of bad water, the land was barren and there were miscarriages and deaths. Elisha received the word or idea from God that he should throw salt into the water and it would be healed. He acted, in faith, on this "odd" idea and God purified the water.

In 2 Kings 4:38-41, we see another occasion when God gave His servant Elisha a "different" idea to solve a problem. A group of prophets had come together for teaching. Elisha sent his servant to prepare a meal of pottage (stew) for them. The servant put a wild vine in the stew. When the men tasted the stew, they immediately knew it was poisonous and cried out to Elisha for help. God obviously gave Elisha the idea that they should add meal to the pot and they did. Somehow, through this simple act of obedience, God miraculously purified the stew.

Another account of an unusual solution to a problem is given in 2 Kings 5:1-14. Naaman, a highly respected military captain from Syria, was mighty in valor and great in his master's eyes because by him the Lord had given deliverance unto Syria, but he had lepropsy. Leprosy was a dreaded, incurable disease.

A little Jewish maid, who had been brought captive to Syria as a child, helped Naaman's wife. She had compassion on her master and told her mistress that there was a prophet in Samaria who could cure Naaman if he would go see him. Naaman decided it was worth investigating so he got together much silver, gold and clothing for the journey, intending to give them to the prophet.

Use your imagination and see Naaman, a mighty man, well respected, bearing valuable gifts, approaching Elisha's house. To his amazement, Elisha stays inside and sends a servant out to give him a message! The servant tells him to go dip himself seven times in the river of Jordan and he will be healed! This was not what Naaman expected, and since he was used to giving orders, he got very angry and said that the rivers of his own country were better than the river Jordan. He left in a rage!

Naaman's servants begged him to do what Elisha said. He finally gave in to their entreaty, went and dipped in the river Jordan. Amazingly, after his seventh dip into the waters, his flesh became like a little child's...all because Elisha, in faith, gave Naaman an "odd" idea from God, and Naaman finally decided to do as he was told.

Even today, God sometimes gives us ideas that don't always *look good* when we first receive them. Remember, the little widow lady in Dr. Cho's church? That land certainly didn't have eye appeal, but God knew what the end result would be IF she followed His guidance. She chose to obey, in faith, and what a return she received for her investment! *God's ideas always work.* They are productive and profitable when we, in faith, obey Him.

A businessman friend, Chuck Reaves, is a very effective seminar speaker. Chuck has written an excellent book entitled *"THE THEORY OF 21."* In it, he states, regarding the world of business, "For every person who will say 'yes,' there are twenty who will say 'no'." He says to get one positive response you must persist through twenty noes!

Chuck has discovered when you present a new idea to a group of twenty-one people, usually twenty of them will immediately find some reason why it can't be done or won't work! His book shows how "play-it-safers" and "do nothings" can effectively sidetrack perfectly wonderful ideas in the business world.

He writes, "These are the people you want to avoid, the nay-sayers who dislike change, fear risk and love ruts, rules and red tape. Learn how to recognize the telltale signs of the 'twenties,' how to avoid or elude them, and how to persevere despite their repeated assurances that whatever you are trying to do won't work. The 'twenty-one' is the 'can do' man or woman, that rare individual who has opened up to ideas and innovations. To be effective, you must find 'twenty-one' and get him or her on your side...attract the 'twenty-ones'...those people who get things done and avoid those people who hold up things."

As I read Chuck's book (available in many Christian bookstores, published by M. Evans and Co., Inc., New York), I thought about how God must feel when He tries to give us wonderful ideas and we avoid them or edit them because we fear change and risks and prefer to stay in a rut rather than risk the unknown that a change would bring. God wants us to be open to His ideas, to be full of faith, not fearful! After reading Chuck's book, I prayed, "Lord, change anything within me that is not open to Your ideas and Your wisdom from above."

Since God made this universe in all of its complexity, variety and wonder, He alone knows the keys, the secrets to running it perfectly. When we are open to His ideas, He will communicate those secrets or ideas to us in every realm. Wherever we have a need, we can operate in His wisdom and knowledge on this earth and live the abundant life that He has planned for all of us. Christians should be so open to Him that they will be the ones who receive His ideas which will bless many on this earth. We must learn to "tap" God's ideas and receive the release of His riches in glory in Christ. Then those who have not believed God is a good God will be drawn closer to Him as they see the fruit of His ideas operating effectively in our lives.

PERSIST WITH FAITH IN GOD'S IDEA.

Early in my Christian walk, I learned the necessity of persisting with faith in God-given ideas. One summer, before my second year in seminary, I had a great financial need. I needed funds to help pay the rising costs of my remaining years in seminary. My earthly father offered to provide the necessary funds but, for personal reasons, I did not feel right about accepting his offer at that time.

I obtained a job as public relations representative for a Boston furniture company. My responsibilities included contacting heads of personnel in large companies in the Boston area. Believe me, that was no easy task! People would respond in the most negative ways.

One day God impressed me to contact the people at a huge nationwide electronics plant. Their head of personnel was a Mr. Whiting and I had phoned numerous times in an attempt to arrange an interview with him. All of my efforts had been unsuccessful. However, that day I felt God wanted me to get in my car and go to this company

43

without an appointment. So I got in my car and drove to this company which was secured like a fortress. They had armed guards in their parking lot!

Right away, I was informed I had to have a little ticket to get in to see Mr. Whiting. Of course, I did not have an identification badge. Sitting in my car, I began to pray. After talking with God, I knew I should walk boldly into the corporation's office headquarter building anyway. So I made my way straight past everyone as though I knew the place and maybe even owned part of it!

Soon I came to a halt in front of a very large secretary who simply sat there and stared at me. I said, "My name is Roxanne Brant. I would like to see Mr. Whiting. I have an idea that will help the many people your company is transferring from the West Coast to Boston for a year of training. The company I work for can provide a furniture rental plan that will meet the needs of your people and also give your company a tax write-off." She looked me straight in the eye and said, "Not interested."

Since it was obvious I couldn't make any headway with her, I went back to my car and prayed, "Lord, I feel like You led me here. This idea was Yours first. What do I do now?" (I discovered later that God was teaching me a lesson in perseverance. His idea would have remained unproductive in my life if I had given up and gone home.) As I waited, deep within my spirit, I heard, "Go again."

Now, I didn't relish going back into those offices and confronting that steel-cold secretary-receptionist. I briefly hesitated, then decided I'd better do as He said. So I got out of my car and again made my way to the secretary's desk. I looked directly at her and assured her I needed only five minutes of Mr. Whiting's time. I was again flatly turned down, so back to my car I went.

About this time, I felt I must be handling the matter all wrong. So I told the Lord it might be a good idea if I left. He said, "No!" After praying about it some more, and not at all happy, I placed one foot in front of the other and went back to the "immovable" secretary.

Standing directly in front of the secretary's desk, I began my third speech by saying, "I know you've seen me before, but let me tell you something about myself this time. I am a seminary student. I intend to enter the ministry and I am not here for selfish reasons. God has put within my heart a compassion for people. The idea He gave me will greatly help your employees and your company. That is why I am here. You have not given me a chance to prove my concern. I ask you to give me a chance!"

She gave me a long look and finally agreed to help me. She said, "Mr. Whiting is due back in his office in approximately 15 minutes. You go over there and sit down. Keep an eye open for a tall, blond man wearing a blue suit and red tie. He has an appointment at 1 P.M., but if you see him coming, follow him into his office, introduce yourself and state your business quickly. I will give you exactly five minutes...no longer!"

Well, she did and I did and my company received a handsome contract from them...and I received a raise in salary.

At the end of the month, my employer sat down with me to evaluate the amount of business transacted. While we were going over the figures, he turned to me and exclaimed, "Roxanne, I don't know how you did it. You have sold more this summer than any of my other sales personnel including my best salesman. In fact, you sold seven times more than anyone else I have ever employed, and you were never even trained professionally, except by me!"

Smiling, I asked him, "Do you want to know how I did it?" Mr. Browne nodded affirmatively. That nice Jewish man didn't know what he was asking for, but I seized the opportunity to share with him for about an hour all about God and His marvelous ideas. I explained that my ideas came from Jesus Christ, that they were not my own. I told

45

him that Christians can tap in to a Source Who will supply their every need. "Mr. Browne," I continued, "God never runs out of ideas. He never fails to give His children ideas that will work when we follow His formula of giving out materially and receiving and walking in obedience to His ideas and words to us. As a seminary student, I have given out materially to the spread of the gospel. As a result, God has given me His ideas to follow and has met my every need."

He listened to every word I said and I noted tears glistening in his eyes. Sensing God's anointing on my words, I explained the way of salvation to him, telling him Jesus is our Savior and our connection to the Father's riches in Heaven. After I had given him the plan of redemption, I shared Philippians 4:19 with him and followed that Scripture with the comment, "Sir, we must never look at our problems. The secret is to look directly to God. We are to focus on Him--not the events taking place around us. On the surface, it appears like the devil and his crowd are running this world. It looks as if evil forces have control of the financial resources in this world. However, when we give God a tithe of our earnings, then Heaven releases a flood of blessings on us. In a sense, we take part of the possessions of this evil world and turn them over to our Father God when we give God part of our material holdings. When we do this, God's resources will explode into our lives. The devil cannot stop the flow of God's blessings upon those of us who obey His Word."

Dear Reader,

Has God given you ideas that have prospered you, after you have given materially to His work? If so, would you share those experiences with us and give me permission to use your experiences as a source of encouragement for others? Of course, we will change names to avoid embarrassing someone. Send your experiences to me and let us give God the glory.

Roxanne Brant, P.O. Box 1000, O'Brien, FL 32071

CHAPTER 4

RICHES...CAN YOU HANDLE THEM?

THE PURPOSE OF PROSPERITY

God has a purpose in prospering us and that is to complete His program of worldwide evangelization. His goal of "preaching the gospel to every creature" should be our goal as well. God intends for His born again, armor-clad army of soul winners to be fruitful and prosperous from the inside outward. We are to be victorious soldiers of Jesus Christ, putting His enemies under His feet. We are to be prospered by the living God, which is the only way the gospel of Jesus Christ can be preached to every creature on this earth (Mark 16:15).

We see this purpose of God in prospering us even under the Old Covenant. God told Moses to tell the Israelites WHY He was going to bless them. The reason God gave still holds true today.

> But you shall remember the Lord your God: for it is He that gives you power to get wealth that He may establish His covenant. (Deuteronomy 8:18)

God wants us to be committed to Him first; then He will bless us financially so we can help evangelize the world with the good news of Jesus Christ before Jesus comes again.

However, in spite of God's tremendous provision, much of the world has still not been evangelized for many reasons. One of the major reasons is because God's children have misappropriated His funds--spending His money on themselves, rather than on Christ's Great Commission of reaching the lost throughout the world.

RICHES ARE NEVER TO BE PURSUED...THEY ARE TO BE RECEIVED!

The clear message of scripture is that man is not able to handle riches or wealth until his relationship with God is right! God tells us when we "seek first the kingdom of God and His righteousness," all of the things necessary for living (with every kind of blessing) will be given to us (Matthew 6:33). We are to set our hearts first on God's kingdom, pursuing God eagerly as our King. When we make this our greatest goal and desire, God will see that everything we need to live the kind of life He intends for His children will be given to us, just as Solomon said:

God has given riches and wealth, and has given man power to eat thereof, and to take his portion, and to rejoice in his labor; this is the gift of God. (Ecclesiastes 5:19)

Someone has said, *"Riches are never to be pursued; they are to be received once we meet God's conditions."*

Many people say they are pursuing God when their actions indicate they are interested only in His dividends, blessings and wealth. In other words, they are pursuing things and that is not right. We must pursue:

THE GIVER--not His gold or gifts.
THE PROVIDER--not His provisions.
THE RELATIONSHIP with God--not His riches.
THE SOURCE of all things--not His supplies.

RELATIONSHIP COMES BEFORE RICHES. If our relationship with God is right, He will give us the material things we need to live in this world. In fact, His Word tells us we will be overtaken with blessings!

And it shall come to pass, if you will hearken diligently unto the voice of the Lord your God, to observe and to do all His commandments which I command you this day, that the Lord your God will set you on high above all nations of the earth: and all these blessings shall come on you, and OVERTAKE YOU, if you will hearken unto the voice of the Lord your God. (Deuteronomy 28:1,2)

Riches and wealth are to be received as dividends of an upright walk with God.

THE BLESSING OF THE LORD MAKES RICH, AND HE ADDS NO SORROW WITH IT. (Proverbs 10:22)

Riches are never to be pursued. In fact, the Bible clearly states that *the deceitfulness of riches and the love of money* are instruments the enemy uses to destroy people.

But those who long to be rich fall into temptation and a snare. They do all kinds of wrong things to get money and give in to many foolish and hurtful lusts, which ruin and destroy them sending them finally to hell. (1 Timothy 6:9 paraphrased)

In other words, people who have such a strong desire to be rich that they begin to *pursue riches,* so they will "possess" many things, will end up trapped by the enemy of their souls. They will do many thoughtless things, give in to hurtful cravings and covetings, and succumb to many foolish and harmful ambitions which will eventually destroy them. Why? The Bible tells us:

For the LOVE OF MONEY is the root (source) of all kinds of evil: which while some have coveted after (were greedy about) they have turned away from the faith, and pierced themselves through with many sorrows. (1 Timothy 6:10 paraphrased)

As an illustration of this, in 1923 nine of the world's wealthiest and most successful financiers attended a very important meeting at the Edgewater Beach Hotel in Chicago, Illinois. These men were obviously very successful at making money. However, in 1948, just twenty-five years later, we find that those same nine men were driven to destruction by money. *They knew how to make money, but they did not know God. Therefore, they were unable to rightly handle the riches they received. Their riches controlled them and eventually drove them to destruction!*

Charles Schwab, a former president of the largest independent steel company in the United States, died bankrupt. Samuel Insull was president of the largest utility company; but he died a fugitive from justice, in poverty, overseas. Howard Hopson, president of the largest gas company, went insane. Arthur Cutten, the most powerful wheat speculator of his time, died insolvent in a foreign land. Richard Whitney, president of the New York Stock Exchange, had been released from Sing-Sing Prison. Albert Fall, once a member of one of our President's cabinets, was mercifully pardoned from prison so he could die at home--penniless. Jesse Livermore, the greatest "bear" on Wall Street, committed suicide. Leon Fraser, president of the Bank of International Settlements, took his own life.

These men knew how to make money but not how to handle it! The Bible clearly tells us if we do not know God and relate to Him intimately through Jesus Christ, our Savior, nothing in our lives will be in right relationship, and we will not be able to handle riches. Instead riches will control us and lead us to destruction. Our goals and priorities must be God's goals and priorities.

50

THE ACCUMULATION AND
DISPENSING OF WEALTH

What is your attitude toward wealth? Wealth can be dedicated to God and His purposes, or we can let it distort our thinking and make us blind to eternal values. Unless we stay "on guard" spiritually, material things can easily dominate our desires and subtly suggest they can provide "security" for us! It is interesting to note that many wealthy people are preoccupied with either losing their wealth or increasing it!

In the midst of the world's philosophy of "GET what you can get out of life," the blazing command of Christ cuts a marked contrast. Jesus said, "Go and GIVE what you can to the people of your day." His command cuts across the entanglements of selfish living. It is a shocking contrast to a godless and commercial society that is involved with a multiplicity of things.

Things, in themselves, are not wrong or evil. It is the desire to pursue wealth that diverts us from the most important eternal and spiritual values in life.

Men have invested all of their energy and abilities in making, manufacturing and marketing an endless array of material things. Ninety percent of media advertising leads to covetousness. From bold and blatant to smooth and sophisticated sales pitches, we are told that *we must have all of the things they are promoting if we want to be happy.* Those are simply lies! We can become caught up in the magnetism of materialism and end up with a mountain of debts! The world urges, "Get." Christ commands, "Give!" *We begin to acquire things and end up controlled by things!* We need to check up on ourselves from time to time to make sure our affections, our priorities and our hearts are centered on Christ--not on things!

Since God made us for Himself, if we give ourselves to things, we miss the mark and purpose of living. But when we respond positively to the claims of Jesus Christ on our lives, we find that He alone holds the secret of eternal life, strength, truth and stability in a shaky, unstable society.

The message of the Bible is that we cannot handle riches apart from being totally committed to God.

THE MAGNETISM OF MATERIALISM

Those who pursue money, letting it be their god, become "sitting ducks" for the enemy of their souls. He then uses all of his persuasive powers to entice them to get more money regardless of what they have to do to obtain it. Regretfully, some who once loved the Lord have had such a strong desire to be wealthy that they have turned away from God and been "wounded with many sorrows and agonies." It has been proven true again and again that whoever trusts in his riches will eventually fall.

He who trusts in his riches shall fall: but the righteous shall flourish as a branch. (Proverbs 11:28)

Paul told Timothy to "flee covetousness, but to follow after righteousness, godliness, faith, love, patience and meekness" (1 Timothy 6:11).

Many people think that since they are financially poor, they will never have a problem with money. However, you can "love money" when you don't have a dime to your name! People who are poor in this world's goods can be as motivated and controlled by their love of money as those who are financially well-to-do!

If you are pursuing wealth instead of pursuing God, you are headed for destruction. As the scripture tells us in Deuteronomy 28:1-2, we need to pursue God. Then His dividends, His blessings, will overtake us while we are obediently following Him.

TRUST GOD...NOT RICHES!

We are to put our trust and confidence in God--not uncertain riches! Paul exhorted Timothy to teach the people entrusted to his care that they should not place their confidence in uncertain riches. He wrote:

> Charge (command) them that are rich in the things of this life, that they should not be proud, nor trust in uncertain riches, but in the living God, Who generously gives us all things to enjoy. Tell them to do good, to be rich in good works, generous and ready to share with others; thereby laying up in store for themselves a good foundation (treasure) against the time to come, that they may lay hold on eternal life. (1 Timothy 6:17-19 paraphrased)

We are a blessed people and this message applies to us today. Just like the early Christians, we need to be reminded that we are to put our trust in the living God Who gives us richly all things for our enjoyment--not in uncertain riches. God is not a miser with white knuckles who grudgingly gives us A FEW THINGS to enjoy. Instead He richly gives us ALL THINGS to enjoy! When will we receive the things He wants us to have for our enjoyment? They begin to come when God sees that we are trusting Him to supply whatever we need, that we are delighting ourselves in Him, and ordering our lives to please Him--not planning how we can acquire things!

The prophet Jeremiah clearly stated God's will when he said:

> Thus says the Lord, "Let not the wise man boast of his wisdom, neither let the mighty man glory in his strength. Let not the rich man glory in his riches: but let him that glorieth glory in this, that he understands and knows Me, that I am the Lord Who exercises lovingkindness, judgment, and righteousness, in the earth: for in these things I delight," says the Lord. (Jeremiah 9:23-24 paraphrased)

53

Those who are well-to-do today must not be proud nor trust in uncertain riches which will soon be gone. Rather they are to trust in the living God Who generously provides everything for our enjoyment. God says those who are rich in this world's goods should practice giving generously from a compassionate heart and sympathize with those who are in distress. If wealthy people will give as God commands, they will accumulate treasures in Heaven for themselves, true riches that will endure forever in the life to come. The Bible also tells us:

> The wealth of the sinner is laid up for righteous men. (Proverbs 13:22 paraphrased)

God wants us to "lend" to many, to share with others, and not borrow (Deuteronomy 28:12). He is a giver and we should be givers too. If we say we are children of God, we should have giving hearts and always be ready to help others. If God is dealing with you about being more open about helping others, cooperate with Him. You will receive rich blessings when you, too, flow in the ministry of giving!

GOD'S PRIORITIES

Paul recorded a most touching account of sacrificial giving by the saints in Macedonia. He wrote about God's grace and the love that prompted those saints to give generously at a time when they were experiencing tremendous trials, difficulties and poverty. Those Christians gave so joyfully that Paul wrote:

> For to their ability, I bear record (witness), yes, and beyond their ability they voluntarily gave, begging us insistently that we would receive their gifts for the relief and support of the saints. And they did this, not as we hoped, but THEY FIRST GAVE THEMSELVES TO THE LORD, AND UNTO US BY THE WILL OF GOD, disregarding their personal interests, giving as much as they possibly could. (2 Corinthians 8:3-5 paraphrased)

Paul said the Macedonian Christians gave well beyond their means and actually earnestly begged him to take their offerings to assist their brothers and sisters in Christ. They indeed exceeded his expectations. Note that *they FIRST gave themselves to the Lord, and THEN to Paul and his company as God's appointed ministers!*

A key to giving is that we must FIRST give ourselves to the Lord. This simple, but important act, puts us in a position to hear from God. Then we can demonstrate His priorities by carrying out His instructions.

The Macedonian Christians first gave SPIRITUALLY: "they gave themselves to the Lord." Then they gave SACRIFICALLY: "beyond their ability." After that, they gave LOVINGLY and EAGERLY: "of their own accord, begging us with much entreaty."

God is greatly pleased when He sees His people giving liberally and lavishly out of His love and grace. He knows when they are giving joyfully to others even while they have personal needs!

Again and again, the Bible presses home that we must first make a total consecration of ourselves to God. The apostle Paul wrote to the Roman Christians:

I urge you therefore, brethren, by the mercies of God, to present your bodies as a living and holy sacrifice, acceptable to God, which is your reasonable, spiritual service of worship. (Romans 12:1 paraphrased)

Paul wrote to the Christians in Corinth:

Therefore, as you abound in every thing, in faith, and utterance, and knowledge, and in all diligence, and in your love to us, see that you are also generous. I am not trying to dictate to you, but want to point out the zeal of others, and to prove the sincerity of your love. (2 Corinthians 8:7,8 paraphrased)

Paul said their gifts would prove the SINCERITY of their love. This makes sense since the Bible teaches that we show our love by our actions.

Our gifts, more than our words, demonstrate just how sincere our love is. True disciples of Jesus Christ are givers and their lifestyles prove it. God is a giver and He wants all of His children to be like Him. God so loved us that He GAVE His only begotten Son, Jesus, to be our Savior (John 3:16). As someone once said, "When you become a Christian, *to LOVE means to GIVE means to LIVE."*

The ESSENCE OF LIVING IS GIVING in every area of life. In fact, Paul said that God wants us to work with our hands so we will have enough to provide for our needs and have some left over that we can use to help people who are in need.

Let him that stole (the thief) steal no more: but rather let him work with his hands, to make an honest living, so HE WILL HAVE SOMETHING TO GIVE TO THOSE IN NEED. (Ephesians 4:28 paraphrased)

God doesn't want just part of us. *He wants ALL of our being committed to Him.* When we are fully committed to Him, He has us, our pocketbook, automobile, house, bank account and everything else that we own and can freely use it in His service.

If you don't believe you are experiencing the abundant life Jesus came to give us, then you should check to make certain your relationship with God is what it should be. When God has first place in your life, then He can trust you with riches knowing you will keep divine prosperity in proper perspective and riches will not destroy you!

THE DECEITFULNESS OF RICHES

Jesus never said that God is opposed to people having possessions. He said God does not want people to put their

56

trust in things. Both Luke and Matthew recorded Jesus' teaching on this subject:

> *A man's life does not consist in the abundance of the things which he possesses.* (Luke 12:15 paraphrased)

> *Don't lay up treasures on earth for yourselves; rather lay up treasures for yourselves in Heaven.* (Matthew 6:19,20 paraphrased)

If we are not as someone has said, "totally His," then we will be tempted to misuse whatever wealth we have and may find ourselves pursuing riches. This can lead to our losing the most important relationship we could ever have-- fellowship with God. Remember, the scriptures teach us that people who desire to get rich fall into temptations, traps and many foolish and harmful desires that plunge them into ruin and destruction (1 Timothy 6:9-10). God alone is our security. Money cannot be trusted!

The writer of Ecclesiastes recognized that wealth can be misused when he exclaimed:

> *There is a sore evil, terrible thing, which I have seen under the sun, namely riches hoarded or stored to the hurt of the owners thereof against a time when they might need them. But those riches are lost through evil travail, a bad deal.* (Ecclesiastes 5:13,14 paraphrased)

This scripture tells us that we can actually hoard riches to our own hurt. Have you ever considered the fact that wealth can be harmful unless it is used as God directs?

In Luke 12:16-21, Jesus tells about a well-to-do man who continued to store up things for himself until the very hour of his death. Probably, some of the people who knew him envied him his riches. But Jesus said he died bankrupt as far as his relationship with God was concerned. And we know that we cannot take material riches with us when we leave this world! (See 1 Timothy 6:7.)

We must make certain we are totally committed to God and His work or we, like others, can fall prey to the habit of grasping and hoarding things. Someone approached John D. Rockefeller and asked him, "Sir, how many millions does it take to satisfy a man?" He quickly replied, "The next one!"

Mr. Rockefeller spoke truly for Scripture says of the man who heaps riches upon himself:

...neither is his eye satisfied with riches. (Ecclesiastes 4:8)

Wealth and riches are deceitful. If we place our trust in them, they will always disappoint us. God is our only sure source of supply so we must put our trust in Him.

BE A CHANNEL... NOT A STOREHOUSE!

God doesn't want us to be STOREHOUSES. We are supposed to be CHANNELS of His blessings to others--not people who hoard material things.

God wants His children to be generous givers like He is. Solomon wrote that the generous person will prosper, and those who bless others will be blessed themselves:

There are people who GIVE GENEROUSLY, and yet PROSPER; and there are those who WITHHOLD more than is necessary, but it tends to POVERTY. The liberal soul shall be made fat: and HE THAT HELPS OTHERS WILL RECEIVE HELP. (Proverbs 11:24,25 paraphrased)

In other words, one person will freely and lavishly give to others and gain even more. Another person will be stingy and come to poverty! *It is a law of God that the generous giver will become prosperous. When we bless others, we put ourselves in a position to be blessed! God wants us to be conduits or channels of His material blessings...not storehouses!*

58

God does not want things to have us. Instead He wants us to be so committed to Him that we can have things. When God has FIRST PLACE in our lives, we can enjoy things without trusting in them! Again, God does not want us to store up things. He wants us to use things and be a channel of His blessings to others.

If we fail to put things in proper perspective, Jesus can say of us as He did of others,

> How hard it is for those who TRUST IN RICHES to enter into the kingdom of God. (Mark 10:24)

The DECEITFULNESS of riches is spoken of repeatedly in the Bible. *Riches are uncertain. They are here today and gone tomorrow. GOD ALONE IS CERTAIN!*

Jesus innumerated five major devices that satan uses to steal God's word out of the believer's heart. One of these devices is the "deceitfulness of riches."

> *Jesus said, "And these are they which are sown among thorns; such as hear the word, and the cares of this world, and the deceitfulness of riches, and the lusts of other things entering in, choke the word, and it becomes unfruitful."* (Mark 4:18,19)

(Note also His remarks concerning affliction and persecution in verse 17.)

It is very important that we pay attention to Jesus' warning that the "deceitfulness of riches" and the "lusts of other things" entering in will choke the word of God out of our hearts and stifle our spiritual growth.

At times you may hear someone say, "I'm not rich in this world's goods so I won't be deceived by riches." But if that person is pursuing after riches, making them his goal in life—instead of a relationship with God—then he is already deceived!

Riches in themselves are uncertain. In time, they can prove to be DECEITFUL, DISAPPOINTING and DANGEROUS. However, when properly handled, riches can be powerfully used by God to fulfill His purposes in this earth and to bring millions of people out of darkness and into God's light and eternal life through Christ. How exciting!

Dear Reader,

Has God given you ideas that have prospered you? If so, would you share those experiences with us and give me permission to use your experiences as a source of encouragement for others? Of course, we will change names to avoid embarrassing someone.

Send your experiences to me and let us give God thanks for His marvelous ideas.

> *Roxanne Brant*
> *P. O. Box 1000*
> *O'Brien, FL. 32071*

Thank you. God bless you.

CHAPTER 5

GOD WANTS TO PROSPER YOU MATERIALLY.

God wants you to prosper materially. After you come into line with His Word spiritually, He wants to bless you financially so that He can get the gospel out to the ends of the world before Jesus returns.

If you seek God the Provider, His provisions will be yours in abundance. God is called *El-Shaddai*. He wants to abundantly bless His children. God is also called *Jehovah-Jireh*, meaning "Jehovah's provision shall be seen" or God is our Supplier.

Because God is so good, He wants us to prosper from the inside out: our spirits, our souls (minds and emotions), and our bodies. He receives glory when we walk in His prosperity.

Divine prosperity is evident in a life that is totally committed to the living God. The entire lifestyle of a Christian should be one of giving--giving out in every area to help others. When we obey His Word and give out, God will fulfill His promises to bless and prosper us--even materially.

No good thing will He (God) withhold from them that walk uprightly. (Psalm 84:11 paraphrased)

WHAT YOU "SEEd" IS WHAT YOU GET.

God's children should have such giving hearts that they look for opportunities to sow generously. Remember His promise that when we give generously, we will reap a bountiful harvest (Proverbs 11:25, Luke 6:38). Then we will have even more to invest in the Lord's work the next time we have an opportunity to do so.

The Bible tells us that God is the One Who gives us seed to sow (2 Corinthians 9:10). We sow the seed and then reap the harvest. The harvest supplies our needs and gives us even more seed to sow in the future unless we let greed take over and "eat our seed," spending it upon ourselves!

There is a continuation, a growing in the ministry of giving and receiving. The Philippian Christians gave once and again to meet Paul's needs (Philippians 4:17). They did not stop with sharing once and neither should we. We should have a *lifestyle of giving*.

Many Christians need to learn to *sow their seed*, to give God something He can work with, so He can give them a harvest in return. We would think a farmer mentally incompetent if he took a sack full of seed, put it in a corner of his barn and then told people he was expecting a harvest from that seed! God has put such a multiplying potential in seeds that a sack full would completely fill his barn with a harvest if it is planted! However, common sense tells us that seed left in a bag will never produce a crop. The seed must be *planted* or it will remain merely a sack full of seed.

We, too, must *plant* our seed. The Bible tells us we should look for opportunities to sow seed in the good soil of good ministries (2 Corinthians 9:6-13, Galatians 6:10).

GIVING GOD HIS TENTH

The Scriptures teach us that *the earth is the Lord's and the fullness thereof* (Psalm 24:1). They also state consistently that God is due a portion (called the "tithe") from all that we receive. From the days of Abraham onward (Genesis 14), the people who believed in God also knew that they were merely stewards of the material goods God entrusted to their care, and ten percent of everything was His and to be set aside for Him. Actually, that is why the Bible speaks only of *paying* God the tithe instead of *giving* it to Him.

And all the tithe of the land, whether of the seed of the land, or of the fruit of the trees, is the Lord's. (Leviticus 27:30)

The Bible speaks of the tithe being set aside from the *first fruits* of the Israelites agricultural produce. Few people today earn their living by farming. So we should first put aside ten percent to pay to the Lord from whatever source of income we have. His tithe should be set aside before we purchase anything for our personal use! God is the divine owner of all things and creator of all people, and we need to give Him due recognition. In fact, the tithe is the minimum we should give Him!

Jesus put His approval on the practice of giving the tithe.

Woe unto you, scribes and Pharisees, hypocrites! You pay TITHE of mint and anise and cummin, and have omitted the more important matters of the law, right and justice, mercy, loyalty and faithfulness. You ought to have done these and not leave the other undone. (Matthew 23:23 paraphrased)

The New Testament also tells us that the ascended Christ, our eternal priest in Heaven, receives tithes.

*And here men that die receive tithes; but there
He receives them, of whom it is witnessed that
He lives.* (Hebrews 7:8)

The widow who gave two mites is an illustration of one whose giving greatly pleased God.

*And Jesus sat opposite the treasury, and saw how
the people cast money into the treasury. Many
that were rich cast in much. And there came a
certain poor widow, and she threw in two mites
(the smallest of coins, about half a penny).
Jesus called His disciples to Him and said,
"Truly, this poor widow has put more in than all
of them who have cast into the treasury; for they
did cast in of their abundance; but she put in all
that she had, even all her living."* (Mark
12:41-44 paraphrased)

This beautiful account teaches us that:

1) Jesus watches our giving with interest, as in
   the case of this widow.
2) Sacrificial gifts, given from a heart of faith
   and love, mean more to God than gifts from
   people who are so wealthy that they can easily
   write a large check and not have to do without
   anything they really want.
3) God looks at our heart to determine our
   motive for giving. The size of the gift is not
   as important as the motive behind it.

The Scriptures tell us to honor the Lord by giving Him the first part of our income. Then His blessings will come to us as promised.

*Honor the Lord with your substance, and with the
first fruits, the TITHE, of all your increase: so
shall your barns be filled with plenty, and your
presses shall burst out with new wine.* (Proverbs
3:9-10 paraphrased).

Malachi, the prophet, wrote to those in his day who refused to bring their tithes to the Lord:

Will a man rob God? Surely not! Yet you have robbed Me. You have robbed Me of the tithes and offerings due Me. (Malachi 3:8 paraphrased)

There is a curse on those who rob the tenth from God. The Bible clearly states:

You are cursed with a curse: for you have robbed Me, even this whole nation. (Malachi 3:9)

Malachi told the Israelites they were cursed because they had robbed God. He went on to tell them God wanted to bless them and told them what they must do to receive His blessings.

"Bring all the tithes into the storehouse, that there may be meat in My house, and prove Me now (test Me) herewith," says the Lord of hosts. "You will see that I will open the windows of Heaven, and pour out on you such abundant blessing that there won't be room enough to receive it. And I will rebuke the devourer for your sakes, and he shall not destroy the fruits of your ground; neither shall your vine lose her fruit before the time in the field," says the Lord of hosts. "And all nations shall call you blessed: for your land will be a good, delightful land," says the Lord of hosts. (Malachi 3:10-12 paraphrased)

How interesting it is that God told the Israelites He would open the windows of Heaven, and pour them out such a blessing that they would not be able to receive it *if they would bring their tithes into the storehouse*. Here again we see our giving out materially can result in the release of God's ideas.

Of course, the expression *open the windows of Heaven* implies abundant showers of rain and, therefore, removal of drought. But this can also mean the tremendous diffusion of God's heavenly blessings and His wisdom, knowledge and ideas--the gift of His Word in magnificent abundance!

We see God's Words, thoughts and ideas likened to showers of rain in Isaiah 55, verses 8-11:

"For My thoughts are not your thoughts, neither are your ways My ways," says the Lord. "For as the heavens are higher than the earth, so are My ways higher than your ways, and My thoughts than your thoughts. For as the rain comes down, and the snow from heaven, and returns not there, but waters the earth, and makes it bring forth and bud, that it may give seed to the sower, and bread to the eater: So shall My word be that goes forth out of My mouth: it shall not return unto Me void, but it shall accomplish that which I please, and it shall prosper in the thing whereto I sent it." (Isaiah 55:8-11)

Truly, as we give materially to God and His purposes, He gives us back His ideas, like the rain that comes down from Heaven and waters the earth...and brings forth seed for the sower and *bread* to the eater.

GOD'S IDEAS WORK...EVEN IN THE KITCHEN!

Sometimes God's ideas are quite simple. Recently I read a *"GUIDEPOSTS"* article by Jim Head,* a successful salesman who lost his job. The president of the company told him he was "too involved with religion and with his family!"

Jim was a "go getter" so he immediately went job hunting. He finally found one but, to his dismay, the company was sold a few days after he was hired and he was again without work! Jim told his wife Judy he hoped God had something else in mind since two doors had closed on him.

66

Jim Head, "Ya-Hoo!," GUIDEPOSTS, October 1985, p. 11.

SHORTLY THEREAFTER, GOD GAVE JIM HEAD A DREAM. Jim said, "In the dream I was in the kitchen making a cake. It was an amazingly vivid dream: I saw myself assembling the ingredients, mixing them, baking them--the recipe was very precise, down to the exact amount of baking soda. When I woke up with a start, just about dawn, it was all so real that I went into the kitchen and started trying to make the cake in a little old bread pan that I found in the cupboard."

Jim felt the combination of ingredients was rather unusual: chocolate chips, cherries, pecans, a special batter, etc. But the cake smelled good, and tasted even better, so he gave a sample to Harry Coley, a neighbor. Harry yelled, "Ya-hoo, that's a terrific cake!"

Another friend suggested Jim bake the cakes in the shape of the State of Texas. He promised to buy a hundred Texas shaped cakes, so Jim began making cakes in the shape of Texas. Now Jim Head has several hundred employees and his company is making hundreds of cakes every day. God has prospered the Heads tremendously.

Jim and Judy give God all the glory and He is continuing to bless them with "ideas" for new cake recipes. God will prosper you, too, if you faithfully give out materially, follow His ideas, and give Him all the glory that He so richly deserves.

TITHING EXPRESSES GOD'S OWNERSHIP.

Tithing shows God's ownership! It is an expression of worship for the believer, as well as an expression of faith in God's promises, His goodness and His Lordship.

Satan often tempts a new Christian saying, "You don't have enough to make ends meet now, so how will you get by when you give a tenth of your income to God?" Of course, the answer is that WHEN YOU GIVE GOD HIS TENTH, HE MULTIPLIES THE NINE-TENTHS YOU HAVE left over!

Tithing is the only commandment that God has given where He has told us to "prove" or "test" His ability to keep His promise. When we give our tithes (really "His tithes") back to the Lord, He will open the windows of Heaven and pour out on us abundant blessings.

God desires to greatly prosper you so your needs will be met, you can help needy people and support ministries that are preaching His word in power throughout this earth. Once your relationship with Him is right, He can abundantly bless you since you will then be able to keep material things in right perspective. You will be a channel--not a storehouse--of His material riches and will help evangelize the world.

God wants you to have things. He just doesn't want you controlled by things. Jesus told Peter:

Truly, I say to you, there is no man that has left house, or brethren, or sisters, or father, or mother, or wife, or children, or lands, for My sake, and the gospel's, but he shall receive a hundredfold now in this time, houses, and brethren, and sisters, and mothers, and children, and lands, with persecutions; and in the world to come eternal life. (Mark 10:29,30)

GOD'S BLESSING MAKES US RICH!

God is your Provider. He wants to bless you *spiritually and materially*. He tells us in His Word:

The blessing of the Lord makes rich, and He adds no sorrow with it. (Proverbs 10:22)

When we think of God making men rich, the first man who usually comes to mind is Abraham. He was very rich in cattle, silver and gold (Genesis 13:2). We are told that God blessed Abraham in all things (Genesis 24:1). One of the first things God did for Abraham was to make him rich--when he could handle riches. God also prospered

Isaac (Genesis 25:11; 26:12), Jacob (Genesis 28:4; 30:27), Solomon (1 Kings 3:13), and Job (Job 42:10) ...as well as others.

God's spiritual and material blessings were evident in every aspect of these men's lives when they gave Him first place in their hearts. The Scriptures tell us that all of them feared God and sought His wisdom. We are also told that the *fear of the Lord* (a reverent and godly fear) *leads to riches, honor and long life.*

By humility and the fear of the Lord are riches, and honor, and life. (Proverbs 22:4)

God's men valued His wisdom more than His material blessings. *God says of His wisdom:*

Riches and honor are with Me; yes, durable riches and righteousness. My fruit is better than gold, yes, than fine gold; and My revenue than choice silver. I lead in the way of righteousness, in the midst of the paths of justice: that I may cause those that love Me to inherit substance; and I will fill their treasuries. (Proverbs 8:18-21)

Paul told the people at Corinth that *Jesus Christ is our wisdom*, righteousness, sanctification and redemption (1 Corinthians 1:30). God wants us to put Him first, to seek His righteousness and wisdom. As we walk with Jesus, led by the Holy Spirit, God will give us riches or wealth as He knows best. If He gives us riches before we are capable of properly handling them, they can destroy us.

For instance, we wouldn't dream of giving a 9 year old boy $1,000! He might buy $1,000 worth of candy with the money and ruin his teeth. Or he might buy a motorcycle built for an adult and seriously injure himself or someone else. Most children are not physically or mentally equipped to handle that much money or a motorcyle made for an adult, and we would not think of giving them something that would harm them or others.

God is more concerned about the welfare of His children than any earthly parent could ever be. He is all knowledge and wisdom, and He wants to bless us abundantly, not destroy us! He does fill our treasuries as we grow in the knowledge of Him and His purposes for our lives. Then riches will not destroy us, but instead we will be channels of His blessings to others and thereby demonstrate His love for them.

The Bible tells us that Jesus Christ became poor, laid aside His heavenly riches, so that we might have everything we need here on this earth. Paul wrote to the Corinthian Christians:

> *For you know the grace of our Lord Jesus Christ, that, though He was RICH, yet for your sakes He became POOR, that you through His poverty might be rich.* (2 Corinthians 8:9)

Those who have seen glimpses of Heaven tell us they don't have adequate words to accurately describe the spectacular beauty, harmony and peace of Heaven. Yet Jesus willingly left the magnificence and glories of that world to come here with no place to lay His head (Matthew 8:20). He became poor so that we could have access to God's abundant resources. Jesus wants us to share the good things God gives us with others and to commit ourselves to support the proclamation of His coming worldwide.

This takes us back to *God's priorities*. I believe you can see why God has said our relationship must be right with Him before He blesses us. He knows that when we are in right relationship with Him, we will properly use the blessings He sends our way. His blessings make us rich.

The psalmist wrote about God, our Creator, *"The earth is full of Thy riches"* (Psalm 104:24). God wants to share His riches with us. His wisdom will lead us to wealth and durable riches, not perishable riches.

God can "drop" an idea, a "witty invention" (Proverbs 8:12) into our minds that will bless others and prosper and

70

enrich us. He literally delights to give us His wisdom, knowledge and ideas when we are in right relationship with Him. When we follow through on His ideas, we will experience tremendous victory and prosperity, both spiritually and materially.

In the beginning, God made everything, so it is His to distribute. His written word tells us we will be held accountable for the way we use what He gives us (Luke 12:48). So we should seek His will in everything we do, and make certain that whatever we give--or do--is done with the motive that we are giving and doing for His kingdom and glory.

>*...whatever you do, do all to the glory of God.*
>(1 Corinthians 10:31)

In this context, let's learn how to release God's ideas into our lives--not just so we might prosper, but so we can be of service to others and promote God's purposes whether or not we prosper materially.

THE RIGHT HEART MOTIVE: SERVE GOD BECAUSE YOU LOVE HIM AND NOT FOR MATERIAL BENEFITS.

I SERVE GOD BECAUSE I LOVE HIM, NOT BECAUSE HE BLESSES ME MATERIALLY. IF GOD DID NOT BLESS ME MATERIALLY, I WOULD GIVE TO OTHERS ANYWAY AND SERVE HIM WITH MY WHOLE HEART! Today, in certain cultures, because of persecution or extreme circumstances, some people don't have the material comforts and prosperity that we have in this country or that God would like them to enjoy.

Previously, for example, in both Old and New Testament times, many believers were persecuted for their faith. Today some are living in near starvation conditions. These people are obviously not serving God to gain financial prosperity! They serve Him because they love Him. Many choose to live in difficult places and circumstances so they can identify with and minister to needy people. These dear children of God choose to live like this here on earth knowing they will be richly rewarded in Heaven.

These people believe the truth of Scripture that *"the sufferings of this present time are not worthy to be compared with the glory which shall be revealed in us"* (Romans 8:18; 1 Peter 4:13). The Bible also says of many believers:

> ...*others were tortured*...*others had trial of cruel mockings and scourgings, yes, moreover of bonds and imprisonment: They were stoned, they were sawn asunder, were tempted, were slain with the sword: they wandered about in sheepskins and goatskins; being destitute, afflicted, tormented; (Of whom the world was not worthy:) they wandered in deserts, and in mountains, and in dens and caves of the earth.* (Hebrews 11:35-38)

Even the apostle Paul wrote that he was *"as poor, yet making many rich"* (2 Corinthians 6:10). Paul chose to be a channel of material and spiritual blessings to others. He lived very simply and passed material blessings on to others.

Mother Theresa, that great and merciful woman of God who is helping the lepers and poor in India, Africa and other places in the world, is a current day example of one who has chosen to take a vow of poverty to identify with the poor and needy around her. Others have done likewise.

Those of us who live in countries where there is an abundance of material things see much covetousness and greed. We need to realize there are certain situations where God will prosper us spiritually and wants us to live simpler lives materially. This is so we can, unencumbered by the cares of "things," be better equipped to do His work. Many missionaries can testify this is true in their work for the Lord.

I believe God wants those of us who have more than we need to live comfortably to give to people who have needs, supporting missionaries, church and evangelistic work with our giving.

ARE YOU WILLING TO SHARE WITH THOSE IN NEED?

The Bible tells us that the apostle Paul took up collections for the poor saints at Jerusalem. The Christians at Corinth were better off materially so he wrote:

> I don't want you to be burdened, while others are relieved of their responsibility. Rather I ask that, since you have more than you need to care for your family, you share with these in need, that there may be an equality. Then when you have a need, others will share with you. It is written: he that had gathered much had nothing over; and he that had gathered little had no lack.
> (2 Corinthians 8:13-15 paraphrased)

When God is blessing us materially, He wants us to share with those in need. Then should the situation be reversed, God wants others to be a channel of blessing to us.

Always remember that divine prosperity begins with a right and rich relationship with our heavenly Father. His life comes into our spirits and flows out through our minds, emotions, bodies and into our material circumstances. We are pilgrims in this world and must never get attached to things! We cannot build our hopes and affections in the trees of this world that are destined for the axe. The Bible tell us everything in this world will be burned up before God establishes a new heaven and a new earth (2 Peter 3:7,10-13).

Paul told the Corinthian Christians that they should be as people who bought but possessed nothing--people not caught up in the affairs of this world--since the present world order is passing away (1 Corinthians 7:30,31). He recognized that Christians had to deal with the world system to a certain extent. Paul was just concerned that the Christians of his day would not allow themselves to be overcome by the business, cares and pleasures in the world and neglect their relationship with God. In fact, he told them that they should live as if they were strangers here since this world system is going to pass away.

Consider this: why invest your time and energy working hard to accumulate material things you do not need when EVERYTHING MATERIAL IS GOING TO PERISH? Isn't it much better to invest your life and material goods in expanding the kingdom of God, and thereby lay up for yourself treasures in Heaven where they will last forever according to Jesus' promise in Matthew 6:20?

If you know you have not had a right attitude toward riches, have not put God first, simply confess that to Him and receive His forgiveness. Your prayer could be similar to this one:

Father God, I come to You in the name of Your precious Son Jesus. I confess that I have sinned in allowing the pursuit of material wealth to come before my relationship with You. I ask You to please forgive me and help me to put my trust in You, not in riches or the pursuit of them.
Father, You love me and gave Your Son for me and others. You continually give us good gifts. I want to be a giver like You, one You can use to channel Your blessings to others. I want to lay up treasures in Heaven--not in a storehouse here. I give You permission to do whatever You need to do in my life to make me willing to share with others. Thank You, Father, that You are going to pour Your ideas into my life after my priorities line up with Yours and help me walk in Your knowledge and wisdom. I will be a channel to spread the good news of Jesus throughout the earth and tell others about Your blessings.
Thank You for forgiving me and giving me a loving, giving heart. With Your help, I will practice giving beginning now. In Jesus' name. Amen.

CHAPTER 6

GOD'S RESOURCES CAN COME TO US THROUGH OTHERS.

When you sow seed in God's garden, sow expecting an abundant harvest. When our Father God gives you an idea, faith will spring up in your heart. Use the faith He has given you and prayerfully move in the direction He indicates taking it one step, one idea, at a time.

Sometimes God moves on the heart of another person to speak out an idea for our benefit or to take some action that will bless us in some way. He may choose to work through an employer, family member, friend or someone we have never met. Regardless of how He chooses to act in our behalf, the end result will always be an abundant harvest!

When you give your tithes and offerings to God's work, don't "box God in" by expecting His ideas to come the same way all of the time. He may drop an idea into the mind or spirit of someone else who is in a position to speak or act in such a way that you will be richly blessed. You are to simply do your part in giving and then "let God be God." It is His responsibility to find the appropriate channels (people) to release His wisdom, knowledge and ideas back to bless you.

RECEIVING GOD'S IDEAS AND BLESSINGS THROUGH OTHERS

For example, several years ago, God told me to start a retreat center in northern Florida where ministers and misssionaries could come to rest and leave refreshed in body, mind and spirit. He indicated this would be the headquarters for my ministry and a retreat center. God showed me it would also be a total living center for retired people who would help with the ministry, and that some young couples would come here to live, work nearby and help us as they could.

He specified that 240 acres of rolling pasture land with beautiful oaks and pines on it was where the Retreat Center, called *Northern Florida Christian Center,* was to be located. The land was not what I would have selected with my natural mind, but I obeyed His instructions. We have been using that location as our headquarters for several years now.

I knew God would begin sending pastors and missionaries to us for refreshment since many of His choice servants literally pour themselves into their ministry and experience "burn out." I also knew that if we offered to let them come here, we would have to provide housing since most of them would not be able financially to provide a retreat place for themselves. So I prayed and asked God to give us a trailer for that purpose. Back then, a single-wide mobile with two or three bedrooms and one and a half baths cost approximately $10,000 and we didn't have that kind of money readily available at that time.

I prayed for a year that God would either bless us financially so we could purchase a mobile home or provide the mobile home itself. Nothing happened! I knew God had impressed me to provide a place for His servants so I wondered, "Why is it taking so long for this mobile home to materialize?"

Finally, it seemed we had our answer. A man offered us his custom-made mobile home located in Texas. However, as our conversation progressed, I realized it was not financially feasible for us to have his mobile home taken apart, put on trucks and transported to Florida. I thanked him for his kind offer and told him that God and we appreciated his giving heart.

I said, "When the Lord does something, it is usually mutually beneficial. The alterations we would have to make to transport the mobile would lessen the value of the home considerably. So I don't believe we should accept your offer." He agreed. So we were back where we started-- no mobile home for God's servants to use.

Several months later, a friend in the ministry called and asked me to drive down to Tampa, Florida to hear a world famous missionary-evangelist. I had been wanting to observe this man's ministry so, since I had a little free time, I drove down for the last service.

Approximately 5,000 people had gathered for the meeting, which was very powerful. We praised and worshiped the Lord and sensed His awesome presence in our midst. Then the evangelist presented the financial needs to meet the crusade budget. He asked us to pray and let God tell us what we should give in the offering. So I asked the Lord, "What do you want me to give?"

Clear as a bell, I heard Him say, "Roxanne, write a check for $100 and put it in the offering. Then I will give you a mobile home for the ministers and missionaries who will be coming to the Retreat Center."

I was amazed! Now since the approximate cost of a mobile home at that time was $10,000, I realized that mathematically speaking I would be getting a 100-fold return for my giving immediately. That's pretty exciting news. I obeyed and put in a check for $100 when the offering was collected...about 8:30 P.M. I felt like a kid at Christmas. I was so excited that I could hardly wait to see how He was going to deliver the mobile!

It was quite late when the service was dismissed, so I decided to stay overnight in the area and drive home the next day. All of the time, I wondered, "Who will God use or how will He deliver the mobile?" I knew He is faithful to keep His promises and that it was just a matter of time before we would have the mobile on the retreat grounds of Northern Florida Christian Center.

Shortly after my return to the Center, the gentleman who had offered us his custom-made mobile, located in Texas, contacted me.

He said, "Roxanne, about 10:30 last night, as I was going to sleep, I got this TREMENDOUS IDEA! God told me to trade my mobile home to a nationwide mobile home dealer who has franchises in Florida and Texas. The Texas office can then transfer the equity I have in that mobile to a dealer in Florida. Then we can select a new single-wide mobile home in this area for the retreat center."

Remember I gave to God's work about 8:30 P.M. *Two hours later, God gave this man a practical idea!* Don't you agree that was rather quick work?

Our friend got so excited about this idea that he immediately went to check on mobile homes at local dealerships. He found one he especially liked and made arrangements for that good looking single-wide mobile to be delivered to the Center a couple of days later, all totally paid for!

We all rejoiced when the mobile home was put in place. That mobile has proved to be a blessing to many ministers and missionaries who enjoyed staying in it. This all came about because I obeyed God by giving materially. In return, He released an idea to a friend, who followed through on it, and we received a tremendous blessing! Sometimes as we give out materially, God gives ideas to others to bless us.

GIVING SACRIFICALLY AND RECEIVING GOD'S BLESSINGS THROUGH OTHERS

A young girl shared with us that she came to one of our crusade services with only a few dollars in her purse. A mechanic had told her shortly before she came that the braking system in her old car was in bad need of repairs. He told her it would cost around $75. She didn't have that kind of money.

At the close of our evening service, the Lord impressed her to write a check for almost everything she had in her bank account--about $50. Taking a leap of faith, she did. Then the Lord gave her an idea. He prompted her to take the car to the gas station even though she did not have the necessary funds in hand right then. The mechanics began work on the braking system. Sure enough, the bill was over $100. In fact, it was over $200. This was considerably more than she had expected.

While the brake work was being done on her daughter's car--but before they knew what the final cost would be--God impressed the girl's mother to give her a blank check for her birthday so she could use it to pay for the brake job. When the daughter told her mother about the much higher cost, she generously told her to go ahead and write the check for the full amount--over $200!

God had another pleasant surprise for this young lady. Her dad called her at work and asked, "What do you need most for your birthday?" She told him the mechanics had advised her to replace all four of her car tires since they were extremely worn. He responded, "That is a good birthday present for you," and immediately wrote out a check to pay for four new tires. Her parents birthday gifts totaled over $400. God is good!

This young lady gave $50 to the work of the kingdom of God. God, in turn, gave her parents ideas that blessed her financially with over $400. This is a simple example of what happens when we obey God by giving out materially. We are blessed in return and God is glorified as well.

DOES GOD DIRECT YOUR BUSINESS?

Most of us have seen catchy bumper stickers reading "God is my co-pilot" or "God owns my business." Yet how many of us can truthfully say God can always count on us to go, do or give anything we have that He needs to further the preaching of the gospel of Jesus Christ, or to help one of His children who has a need? If you are in business for yourself, do you ask Him for ideas and guidance in giving and then follow His directions? Or if you are planning to start a business, have you asked His advice? He's the best business counselor available!

Walter and Hattie Block, two beautiful people could have answered "Yes" to the above questions. (Walter has now gone on to his rewards in Heaven.) We met Hattie in Wisconsin, where she now lives. We were greatly blessed when she shared with us how God had prospered their business. Hattie is one lady who is full of exuberance and the energy of the Lord!

We learned from Hattie that Walter was fairly well established as an accountant by the time he was 30. He was faithful to the Lord and God blessed Him. Their lifestyle was one of continual loving and giving to help others and to extend the gospel of Christ worldwide.

One day Hattie got *an idea* that they should start a business of making curtain stretchers. They prayed together and agreed the idea was from God, so they made plans to begin the Quaker Curtain Stretcher Company in 1935.

Business competition was strong, but God gave Walter some amazing ideas which resulted in a superior product which they called the "Quaker Ballpoint Stretchers." Their design ideas were far superior to those of other manufacturers, so their profits began to soar!

However, after the war, synthetic curtain materials were introduced on the market and those new curtains didn't need stretching! Almost overnight their sales hit bottom and the Blocks were faced with a serious financial crisis. That did not affect Walter's love for and commitment to God, nor did the Blocks stop giving to finance the gospel and help others. They continued to give large amounts to their church and to sponsor large, interdenominational, city-wide, evangelistic rallies. Also, since the Blocks were concerned about the spiritual welfare of their employees, they continued with their spiritual enrichment program during the employees' lunch hour.

Walter was totally dedicated to the Lord. He believed God would show him what he should do next. *He knew that all he needed was another idea from God.* So during those difficult days, Walter turned to the Lord and asked Him for another idea. He asked God what product they should manufacture.

By this time, television has been on the market for several years, but the Blocks did not own a set themselves. One day, a young Christian friend, who was active in the evangelistic rallies that Walter had begun and was supporting financially, came to Walter with an idea. He said, "Walter, you need to manufacture television tray tables." Television tray tables were already on the market and were very popular.

Walter prayed about this idea and researched the feasibility of Quaker producing television tray tables. A year before, Walter had purchased a very expensive piece of equipment to use in producing the products they were then manufacturing. He discovered that, with very minor changes, he could modify and use that expensive piece of equipment to manufacture television tray tables.

The Blocks continued to give to further the gospel message and help others, and Walter followed through on the many ideas God gave him for different kinds of tray tables. Eventually, Quaker became the leading manufacturer of tray tables--as well as several other products *all because He followed God's ideas!*

One of the ideas God gave Walter was that he should purchase and store large amounts of certain materials. He followed through on the idea. That idea proved immensely valuable to Quaker Industries since the materials he bought and stored were very difficult to obtain during and after World War II. Since Quaker Industries had the necessary materials, their company became the largest supplier of

Army cots during World War II in addition to their being able to continue making tray tables!

Walter and Hattie continued giving to the work of the Lord and helping others. In return, God kept giving him a continual flow of ideas to bless them and Walter decided to give even more to God. So they assigned the patents for the new designs to the Quaker Foundation. All of the royalties from the patents went to the foundation. Funds from the foundation have been used to propagate the gospel of Jesus Christ worldwide, bless many people materially, and promote educational projects as well.

If you are in business, have dedicated your life and business to God, and are living and giving the way He wants you to live, then your business is His business. God will give you ideas and walk with you through every problem that comes against you personally or your business. As you follow His guidance, He will bless you even more than He already has, and you will become a businessman or businesswoman for God!

Always remember the Blocks' example of faithfulness in commitment and giving to God in the midst of adversity. No matter what kind of financial crises, problems and difficulties come against you, remain steadfast in your commitment to God and He will give you ideas that will bring you through triumphantly. (See Psalm 34:19; 2 Timothy 3:11,12; Job 42:10,12.)

THE HOLY SPIRIT BRINGS GOD'S IDEA, AND LIFTS UP THE STANDARD OF HIS WORD IN OUR BATTLES.

The prophet Isaiah recorded a beautiful promise for us.

When the enemy shall come in, like a flood the Spirit of the Lord shall lift up a standard against him. (Isaiah 59:19)

Some people interpret this verse to mean that our enemy comes in like a flood. I believe the Spirit of the Lord comes in like a flood, lifting up God's standard against our enemy and puts him to flight! The Holy Spirit delights to give us the wisdom of God, His knowledge and His word that we need to overcome each time the enemy attacks us. He will speak a word or idea into your heart. If you follow through, you will experience His victory in every problem that comes against you.

It is sad, but true, that many Christians have a "nodding" acquaintance with God when things are going well for them. However when everything looks "topsy-turvy" in their lives or they find they are overwhelmed by problems, they immediately yell, "Help, God!" God is such a good loving Father that He does not turn His children away, but responds to their cry, giving them the help, strength and ideas that they need to overcome their problems.

Being "mature in the Lord" does not make one immune to problems either. In fact as we cooperate with the Lord to bring about His kingdom on earth, we will be taking territory (and people) from the devil's kingdom. That makes him extremely angry and he will wage war on us! Be assured that all believers experience problems and tests of one kind or another; but as we remain faithful to God, pray, give, feed on His word and live according to His Word, He will give us ideas that will solve all of the problems that come against us. Praise the Lord!

The tests and trials that come into our lives should cause us to draw closer to God, listen more keenly to what He has to say about the situation, and then follow His advice which never fails! God's ideas produce faith in us, but we must verbalize the idea He gives us and walk it out if we want to put the enemy to flight.

God's ideas are powerful. They will change people and situations. God is the only One who can turn our mistakes into victories. He does that by changing us and giving us His wonderful, creative, victorious and exciting ideas.

GOD HAS BIG IDEAS!

God has big ideas--we just need to "plug in." Those who do "plug in" can testify that this is true.

I have observed this beautiful truth in operation in the lives of Rev. and Mrs. Glen Cole for several years. I met Glen and his lovely wife Mary Ann early in my ministry and first ministered with Glen when he was pastoring a large church in Olympia, Washington. Over the years, I have watched Glen give generously materially and have sensed his concern for world missions.

In May of 1978, Glen accepted the pastorate of Capital Christian Center in Sacramento, California, then known as Bethel Temple, a church that would seat comfortably about 1,500--but was averaging approximately 700-800 in regular attendance at their Sunday morning services. Glen preached the Word of God faithfully, pastored his people and freely gave to the work of the kingdom. God blessed his efforts.

Many people began coming to the church services. In no time, the sanctuary was filled to capacity. God's blessings on the church were evident. Soon the leaders realized they needed to acquire a site where they could build a much larger sanctuary.

About this time, a forty acre piece of land, part of a 250 acre site (owned by three gentlemen connected with the church), was brought to the attention of Pastor Cole. One of the men came to see the pastor about this property. He said, "Do you think this is the best piece of land we could obtain on which to build our church? Are you satisfied that this site is God's best for our church?"

To his amazement, Glen heard himself say, *"YES, I THINK IT IS. AND I THINK YOU SHOULD MAKE IT A GIFT TO THE CHURCH BECAUSE WE NEED A MIRACLE!"*

Glen's remark probably stunned this Christian businessman for he stood up and prepared to leave before Glen could ask permission to pray with him. On his way out of Glen's office, he said, "I'll call you."

Sure enough, at 10:30 the next morning Glen's phone rang. This Christian real-estate developer was on the line. He simply announced, "It's yours."

In telling me about this experience, Glen said, "I have never said anything like that to anyone in my life, but it came out of my mouth that day! And God gave us a $2 million dollar miracle."

Obviously, the idea to give the land came from God. It truly surprised Glen as much as the man to whom it was directed! But the important thing is that when the man presented this idea to the two other businessmen, they received the idea as being from God, accepted it and acted on it. Only $360,000 was needed to finalize the entire deal on this freeway property. The church gladly paid!!

After plans had been made to develop the property, one of the three businessmen called Rev. Cole. He said, "Don't say anything. Just come with me." He took Glen to a sixty-eight acre site located on the major freeway southeast of Sacramento but four and a half miles closer to the city than the forty acre site which was located on the same freeway.

He told Glen the sixty-eight acre site had been set aside for a highway interchange, but no money was available for development, so the State of California had put it on the auction block. He was the only bidder and his bid was accepted. This real estate developer told Glen he felt the sixty-eight acre site was a much better location for their church. He offered, "You take the sixty-eight acres and I will take the forty acres. I can use the forty acres for industrial purposes so I will let the church have this land in an even exchange. I'll trade you...even up."

This offer sounded advantageous to both sides. Glen presented it to the board and, after prayer, they unanimously agreed that the new acreage was definitely the best site and God's will for the church.

God has blessed these businessmen-partners even more for their obedience in giving the large site to the church. Their businesses continue to prosper and grow, and all of these men are well respected within the community. Because they gave, God raised up a marvelous complex on a magnificent site. The church complex is presently valued in excess of $25,000,000 and approximately 5,000 people regularly attend services there. The people continue to praise God for what He has done for them.

Glen told me that during their building program, God impressed him they should give a tithe to missions on all the money that was given specifically for their new church facilities. The church agreed and obediently gave large sums of money to missionary outreaches even though they had many pressing financial needs in their huge building program.

The goal of the church is to pay off the building indebtedness in five years. When their church is debt free, the people at Capital Christian Center plan to give fifty percent of their income to home and foreign missions!

Many people wish God would give them BIG ideas and release million dollar gifts and blessings upon them or their projects. However, they need to first realize that God blesses those whose lifestyle is one of living and giving as He commands. That's why Rev. Glen Cole and the members of Capital Christian Center received such a big financial miracle. They are big givers! Their vision and actions agree with God's--that the sharing of the gospel of Jesus Christ is of utmost priority.

If other people would give faithfully and generously to support the preaching of the gospel of Jesus worldwide--and help others as they have opportunity to do so--God would delight to bless them with ideas that would enrich them. Then they would be even better equipped to help propagate the gospel and bless many people.

God is looking for people He can trust to be channels of His blessings to multitudes of people! As Glen says, *"GOD IS A GOD OF BIG IDEAS IF WE 'PLUG IN.' THERE IS NO LIMIT TO WHAT GOD CAN DO."* Hallelujah!

PROMOTION COMES FROM GOD.

God is always faithful to His Word. He has promised to bless all of us who faithfully keep His commandments of loving, giving and living to please Him. His methods of delivery will vary depending on circumstances around us. A Christian employer who listens to the Lord will receive ideas from God designed to bless and prosper his or her faithful employees, and will enjoy doing so.

You may ask, "What about those who are working for people who do not believe in Jesus or God?" Never forget: God created this universe and He is running it! Even though our circumstances might not look good at the present time, He has everything under control! Consider the Biblical account of how He advanced Joseph to an extremely important position in a foreign culture. God tells us to be faithful and He will see that we are promoted.

> ...*promotion does not come from the east, nor from the west, nor from the south. But God is the judge: He puts one down and sets up another.* (Psalm 75:6,7 paraphrased)

God simply speaks to Christians and non-Christians in different ways. He delights in dropping ideas into the spirits of Christians (Proverbs 20:27) and into the minds of non-Christians.

If your employer doesn't believe in God, that doesn't stop God from dropping ideas into his or her mind. Haven't you heard of an employer saying something like this, "Henry, I've been thinking what a good employee you have been. You've been faithful and honest, so I've decided to give you a raise and promotion. What do you think about that?"

Now, Henry's employer probably wouldn't think of giving God the credit for his "thought" to promote Henry. He also probably doesn't know about Henry's charitable giving since Henry hasn't mentioned it. But God and Henry know why Henry is getting a raise and being promoted...because Henry gave out materially to help others and God released an idea that would prosper Henry!

The Bible gives us an account of a night when God kept a powerful heathen king awake so he could use that king to bless Mordecai, one of His faithful servants, and bless the Jews. (You can read the story in Esther 6:1-11.)

Our responsibility is to simply obediently and faithfully live and give as He tells us. God will take care of finding a way to release His ideas and blessings into our lives. He wants us to live with an attitude of expectancy and give Him the glory when He blesses us.

Always remember, we are not to "hoard" His material blessings. He doesn't want us to give once, receive His ideas and blessings and then stop giving. Giving is a lifestyle for the Christian! The more we continue to give, the more we will continue to receive. God blesses us so we can bless many others. He delights to give good things to His children and is pleased when His children are givers...like Him!

Dear Reader,

Has God given you ideas that have prospered you, after you have given materially to His work? If so, would you share your experiences with me? Send them to me:

Roxanne Brant, P.O. Box 1000, O'Brien, Fl 32071

CHAPTER 7

WALKING AND WORKING TOGETHER WITH GOD

When you seek closer fellowship with God, walking and working together with Him, He will instruct and guide you in all the affairs of your life.

Many people think it will be easy to walk out an idea that God gives them, and that they will prosper instantly. But people often:

1) become proud when an idea leads to an increase in their material goods,
2) forget God and depend on riches or
3) attribute the blessings they receive to some source other than God.

When God's blessings come your way, so do TESTS! God spoke through His servant Moses to tell the Israelites they should be careful not to forget Him after He had blessed them with a good land that had everything they needed: productive soil, good water, plenty of food and well built houses.

Beware that you do not forget the Lord your God, and thus fail to keep His commandments, His judgments, and His statutes which I command you this day.

For if you do, when you have eaten and are full, and have built fine homes, and dwell therein; and when your herds and your flocks multiply, and your silver and your gold is multiplied, and all that you have has multiplied; then you will become proud, and you will forget the Lord your God, Who brought you out of the land of Egypt, from bondage; Who led you through that great and terrible wilderness, wherein were fiery serpents, and scorpions, and drought, where there was no water; Who gave you water out of the rock of flint; Who fed you in the wilderness with manna, unknown to your fathers, that He might humble you and prove or test you, and later prosper you. And you will think in your mind, "My efforts have brought me this wealth."

You must remember the Lord your God: for IT IS GOD WHO GIVES YOU POWER TO GET WEALTH so He may establish His covenant which He promised to your fathers. (Deuteronomy 8:11-18 paraphrased)

God tests us to determine if we will properly relate to the good things He has promised and will continue to remember that He is our Source, depending on Him and being obedient to Him.

When tests come our way, we have to decide whether we will follow God's instructions, the pull of our own fleshly desires, or listen to suggestions from satan. These tests reveal any weakness within us to which satan can appeal. We have to pass many of God's basic and fundamental tests, such as His tests in the area of material giving, BEFORE He will trust us to function in greater areas with Heaven's wisdom, revelations, ideas and blessings.

Jesus said that WE MUST BE FAITHFUL FIRST IN THAT WHICH IS LEAST--our material giving--BEFORE GOD WILL COMMIT TO US HEAVEN'S TRUE RICHES! In Luke 16:10 and 11, we read His words:

He that is faithful in that which is least is also faithful in much. He who is unjust in the least is also unjust in much.

90

If therefore you have not been faithful in the unrighteous mammon (your material giving to God), who will commit to your trust the true riches?

It is only as we are faithful to give God His due--pay our tithes--and give offerings as He leads us to help others, that we can expect to receive back Heaven's true riches, Heaven's ideas and blessings to help us live productive, fruitful lives for God's glory.

GOD TESTS US IN THE AREA OF GIVING.

God tests us in the area of giving before He gives us that which is most valuable to Him--Heaven's revelations and blessings!

A wise, older minister friend of mine, experienced this vividly in his own life shortly after the Depression. Kenneth was pastoring a small, struggling, but growing, church in Texas in 1940. Kenneth's weekly wages were about $10 and he was trying to save up enough to buy Christmas gifts for his family. (At that time, $10 was equivalent to about $200 in buying power. One could live on $40 per month!)

Just before Christmas, a man who had only recently begun holding evangelistic meetings--we'll call him "Charles"--came to the services at Kenneth's church. He and his family of 6 were visiting his wife's family, members of Kenneth's church, during this slack time in their ministry. Kenneth asked Charles to speak, thinking he would give him $5, the usual offering, but Charles was too embarrassed to speak in front of his family. So Kenneth brought the message and then went to the back of the church to greet the people.

While Kenneth was shaking hands with the people, and Charles, God told Kenneth to give Charles the $10 he had been saving. Now, he didn't want to but, after an inner

91

struggle--and all the time smiling and shaking hands with the people--Kenneth decided to obey God.

Kenneth got together change and enough bills to make up $10 and then went outside where the young evangelist was talking with a friend. He shook hands with Charles and left the money in his hand.

Shortly after Christmas, Kenneth overheard Charles' mother-in-law telling someone, "You know, Charles was off at Christmas time, and he had just enough to pay his rent and utilities. He didn't have a dime left--not a dime. He couldn't buy the kids anything for Christmas, or even any Christmas dinner. Somebody gave him $10 so they had Christmas dinner."*

Kenneth didn't say anything to anyone about what he had done, but when he heard those words, he said in his heart, "Thank You, God. I'm so glad I obeyed You."

A few years later, still in the post Depression era, a similar thing happened in Kenneth's ministry. His church was located right beside the highway that the buses used. One Sunday evening, shortly before time for their service to begin, a Greyhound bus pulled up and stopped in front of his church. A minister that Kenneth recognized got off with his suitcase. Kenneth welcomed him and asked him to preach that evening.

While this minister--whom we'll call George--was preaching, God told Kenneth to give George the $12.50 he had in his pocket. That was more than Kenneth was making a week and he argued with God all during George's sermon. He still wasn't enthused about giving George the $12.50 when the service ended!

He felt he should invite George to spend the night with them, so he did. Kenneth knew he should obey God so, in obedience, he began to count out $12.50 mostly in nickels, dimes and pennies! While he was counting the money, God revealed to Kenneth that George was broke, in between churches and very needy.

92

Kenneth Hagin, "Obedience in Finances," THE WORD OF FAITH, September 1982, p. 8

Kenneth gave George the $12.50 in change and bills and George confirmed that he was indeed broke, didn't have a dime to his name, and had gotten off the bus at Kenneth's church because he didn't have the money to pay his fare any farther!

About two years after Kenneth gave George the $12.50, a church member asked Kenneth and his wife to go and minister to a woman who had been given up to die by doctors at three Texas clinics. All of the doctors had told her husband she had an incurable blood disease (along with other problems). She was too far gone for medical help and they said she would be dead in a few days.

Kenneth and his wife drove to the sick woman's home to pray for her healing. As they were kneeling beside her bed, praying, Kenneth had an amazing experience. He said:

> As we knelt by this woman's bed, the same voice that had told me to give the one minister $10 and the other $12.50--that inward voice--said, "Get up and stand up. Don't pray." (I already had my hand on her head and was praying. My wife was kneeling right by me.)
> "Don't touch her. Get up and stand up, and say to her, 'The Lord told me to tell you you're healed. Get up.'"
> On Thursday she was raised up from her deathbed and on Sunday she was over at our church dancing and shouting the victory!
> As we returned home down old Highway 24, rejoicing that God had used us to raise up a woman from the deathbed, just as plainly as if somebody were sitting in the back seat, the Lord said to me, "I couldn't have used you today if you hadn't obeyed Me on that $10 and that $12.50." I'd forgotten it. I had to stop and think, "WHAT DO YOU MEAN, THAT $10 AND THAT $12.50?"
> "That $10 you gave Brother C. and that

$12.50 to So-and-so." (The evangelist and then
the pastor who was between churches.)
      "Yes," I said, "I remember that."
      "If you hadn't obeyed Me on that, I couldn't
have used you here," the Lord said.*

Of course, we all want God to use us. We want God
to use us to raise someone up from a deathbed, to pull
people out of wheelchairs and to see the sick healed
miraculously. But how are we going to know if it is God
telling us to tell people to get up from a deathbed or to
come out of a wheelchair if we don't know His voice
when He tells us to give $1, $5 or $100? One of the
ways we start learning God's voice is by obeying Him in
the area of giving, in the small, foundational things.

According to Luke 16:10 and 11, if God can't trust
us to obey and respond to Him with $5, $10 or $100,
how can He trust us with Heaven's revelations or to raise
somebody up from their deathbed?

As we obey God in small things, passing the tests of
obedience, He trusts us with bigger things. We become
more fruitful and a more powerful channel of His blessing
as we walk and work together with Him.

God already knows the condition of our hearts, what
we are really like, so He doesn't have to test us to
determine that. He permits circumstances to come into
our lives so we can see what is really in our hearts.
The Biblical account of King Hezekiah is just one example
of a time when God removed the awareness of Himself
from a person to test his character, to see if he would
obey or disobey Him. God can do the same thing with
us.

When the Babylonian ambassadors came to inquire
about the wonder that was done in the land, God
left him (Hezekiah), to try or test him, that he
might know all that was in his heart. (2
Chronicles 32:31 paraphrased)

94

Kenneth Hagin, "Obedience in Finances," THE WORD OF FAITH, September,
1982, p. 9.

AN IDEA FROM GOD THAT
REACHES AROUND THE WORLD

While ministering recently in California, God dropped a beautiful idea into my spirit. The more I prayed, the more the idea "grew." I told the Lord I would do what He said and the idea literally became a part of me and a "heartbeat" of this ministry.

The idea He gave me was simply this: the missionaries who are serving Him in foreign countries long to know what the Holy Spirit is saying to the Church around the world today. He indicated many missionaries feel very isolated and discouraged, far from their native lands, relatives and friends. God told me that His missionaries need inspired, encouraging materials, filled with *current revelation* from His word.

God said, *"MY MISSIONARIES KNOW WHAT I HAVE SAID IN MY WORD, but THEY are hungry to know, and NEED TO KNOW WHAT I AM SAYING TODAY, BY MY SPIRIT, TO MY CHURCH AROUND THE WORLD."*

I knew that missionaries have Bibles. I also knew from my travels that many people desire to know what God is saying to His people today. Since these missionaries are on the frontlines of battle, doing His work, I knew we need to encourage them with letters, our prayers and gifts. However, this idea reminded me that we also need to give them something fresh from His Word.

God told me to send a book or booklet and cassette tape each month to missionaries. The words *"FRESH MONTHLY MANNA FOR MISSIONARIES"* kept coming to me. So I said, "Thank you, Lord, for this idea and program; however, our ministry has financial needs and must pay off several large notes now, so how about if we wait two or three months to begin this outreach to missionaries?" He replied, "Begin to plan and send these packets *now* (within 45 days)." He assured me that as we gave out of our need, He would bring even more into our ministry to support it as well. His words were clear and I accepted them.

I calculated that it would cost us approximately $5,000 a month to follow through with His idea. I received the idea, evaluated it, and asked the Lord for another idea as we didn't have $5,000 extra in our account to underwrite sending these materials to missionaries! He gave me a "management idea," one that would bring in at least some of the necessary capital to finance this outreach.

He told me to write to the people on our mailing list and tell them what He had shared with me about His missionaries needing encouraging, inspirational materials so that they could know what the Holy Spirit is saying to the Church today. Since God showed me that it would cost us about $60 per year to send monthly inspirational materials to each missionary (or missionary couple), I shared this with the people on our mailing list. They responded by wanting to sponsor missionaries receiving inspirational literature under this plan. Now we have several hundred people each sponsoring one or more missionaries in 86 different countries worldwide. PRAISE THE LORD!

God gave me the initial idea of this program. He gave me a subsequent idea of how to manage the program. Then He impressed His children to send in the funds we need to carry out the program.

I have walked with God from idea to idea in many different areas. I have found His ideas always work. We are now receiving many letters from missionaries around the world saying that they greatly appreciate all the materials we have sent, that they have been blessed and enriched by them. Many mentioned that they are eagerly awaiting the next packet of inspirational materials. It is wonderful to get an idea from God that enriches others. We must learn to obey God and keep giving out *faithfully and consistently* to help others--whether we give at times out of our abundance or out of our need!

In 1 Kings 17:8-16 God commanded a widow woman to sustain the prophet Elijah--during a time of drought and starvation!

And the word of the Lord came unto him (Elijah)
saying, "Arise, go to Zarephath...and dwell
there. I have commanded a widow woman there
to feed you."

When Elijah came to the gate of the city, he saw
a widow woman gathering sticks. He called to
her and said, "Bring me, I pray you, a little
water in a vessel that I may drink." As she was
going to get it, he called to her and said, "Bring
me, I pray you, a morsel of bread in your
hand."

She said, "As the Lord your God lives, I do not
have a cake, but only a handful of meal in a
barrel, and a little oil in a cruse. See, I am
gathering two sticks that I may go in and prepare
it for me and my son that we may eat it and
die."

Elijah said to her, "Fear not. Go and do as
you have said, but first make me a little cake
and bring it to me, and afterwards make cakes
for you and your son." (1 Kings 17:8-13
paraphrased)

Notice that Elijah told her to not fear but to be obedient to the Word of the Lord, to make him, "a little cake
FIRST," and then, AFTER that, to make a cake for herself
and her son (verse 13). Then God gave His Word to Elijah
to benefit the woman. What a tremendous revelation! God
said that because she had given, *"The barrel of meal will*
not be empty, nor the cruse (jar) of oil fail until the day
that the Lord sends rain upon the earth." (verse 14)

AFTER the widow gave, God's material blessing was
multiplied to her.

She did what Elijah said and they never ran out of
food. The barrel of meal was never empty and
the cruse of oil did not fail, just as the Lord

promised her through His servant Elijah. (1 Kings 17:15,16 paraphrased)

BE A CHANNEL OF HELP AND HOPE TO OTHERS.

GOD HAS A PLAN AND PURPOSE FOR YOU! It is up to you to discover His purpose for you and how He wants you to contribute to the expansion of His kingdom on this earth. I pray that you will always choose to walk obediently with God, Who gives us ideas, in such a way that He will receive much honor and glory. I also pray that when He prospers you materially you will not let your material blessings possess you, but will instead let God use you as a channel of help and hope to others.

In counseling many people about how to begin giving, I tell them, "Make sure that you pay your tithes." I also tell them, "Begin giving offerings on whatever level you can at the present time." It is a good idea to prayerfully consider, let's say, five ministries God has used to bless you most in your life. Then start by giving a small amount, if that is all you have, to each on a monthly basis. One person that I know began by giving $2 each to 5 different ministries that had blessed him powerfully. Begin giving, whatever you can, in a consistent way, to those ministries that have blessed you. Then ASK GOD TO HELP YOU INCREASE YOUR GIVING and make you a giver.

Though God gives many different kinds of ideas to solve problems and relationships, physical diseases or circumstances, we have concentrated more here on ideas that will produce material prosperity. The Christian has to prosper materially before the Church can prosper and get the gospel out to all the nations of the earth before Jesus comes. I know the teaching in this book is not exhaustive. However, I pray these concepts that God has given me will prove helpful to you who want to be more obedient to Him and bare much more fruit for His glory.

Prayer for Salvation

If you have never asked God to forgive you for your sins and invited Jesus to come into your life and be your Lord and Savior, you need to because the Bible says, "all have sinned and come short of the glory of God" (Romans 3:23). God sent Jesus to be your SAVIOR. He gave His life on the cross for your sins so you could receive God's forgiveness and eternal life.

Pray this prayer asking God to forgive you and Jesus to come into your life. He will if you ask Him (Revelation 3:20).

Dear God, I admit that I am a sinner and need Your forgiveness. Your Word tells me that Jesus died on the cross so we can be reconciled to You. I believe that Jesus is Your Son and that He died for me. Because of what He did, I ask You to forgive me of my sins and cleanse me.

Jesus, thank You for giving Your life for me. I ask You to take control of my life so that I can live a life that will be pleasing to You and God. I want my life to bring glory to You and God. You said if we ask, believing, we will receive, so I thank You that I am now forgiven and can call God my Father. Thank You for accepting me.

If you prayed the above prayer for the first time, let me know and we will send you some helpful reading material. Ask God to help you find a church in your area where the people believe the Bible, truly love one another, and where the leaders lives demonstrate their faith in God's Word. Worship there regularly so you can grow spiritually and bless others.

Roxanne Brant

Cassettes by Roxanne Brant

Order cassettes by listing number on Clip Out Order Form

$5.00 PER CASSETTE

____RB 040 *Ministering To The Lord*

A VISION OF JESUS WEEPING IN THE MIDST OF HIS PEOPLE. The Church's and the Christian's ministry is *first,* to the Lord, *second,* to the saints, and *third,* to the world. (1) How God has created man for His pleasure and to fellowship with Him. (2) How Christians are a "royal priesthood" (I Peter 2:9) with their first ministry to God. (3) How all ministry and blessing on our Christian work must necessarily flow from our ministry to the Lord. (4) Ministering to the Lord involves praise, worship, communion. The difference between praise and worship. A VISION, A SEARCH AND A DISCOVERY. (SEE BOOK BY SAME TITLE).

____RB 042 *How To Develop Spiritually*

After we come to Christ, we develop spiritually by doing 3 things: (1) MEDITATING ON GOD'S WORD - the difference between reading the Bible and meditating on its contents. (2) PRACTICING GOD'S WORD -you will never know the meaning of Jesus' words until you go and DO what He says to do. (3) SPEAKING GOD'S WORD CONSISTENTLY. A discussion of the tremendous creative power of the Holy Spirit and the Word of God working together to change us and change situations as we do the three things mentioned above.

____RB 044 *My Spiritual Journey*

Miss Brant, born into an economically and culturally privileged family, had no religious upbringing. She relates her conversion experience (when she saw Jesus in a university library) which sounds much like a recounting of Acts 9 when Paul was converted on the Damascus Road. Also, she shares her experience of being baptized in the Holy Spirit, and the day that Jesus appeared to her and her healing ministry began.

____RB 046 *The Prophetic Ministry*

One of the five ministries set in the church by Christ. To have a prophetic ministry, one must be (a) a minister called by God and (b) have at least 2 of the 3 revelation gifts of the Spirit, plus prophecy operating in abundance in his life. A prophet has visions and revelations; sees and knows things supernaturally. A discussion of some Old and New Testament prophets, personal prophecy then and now, with examples and scriptures: Ephesians 4:11, I Cor. 12:7-10 and I Cor. 12:27-31. (See cassette #RB 010 and RB 012, How To Test Christian Ministry and Guidance, as well as the book, "How To Test Prophecy, Preaching and Guidance," for related teaching).

___RB 048 *Dying To Live*

A powerful message on Romans 6, including a vision and dream from Jesus in which He said, "Relax and believe - it's already been done." Three deaths are predicated of the Christian believer, Romans 6, 7 and 8. (1) We are dead to sin...and alive to God (Rms. 6:11). (2) We are dead to the law...and married to Christ (Rms. 7:4). (3) We are dead to the flesh...and led by the Spirit (Rms. 8:13). Therefore (1) KNOW THIS (2) RECKON YOURSELVES DEAD TO SIN AND ALIVE TO GOD (3) YIELD YOURSELVES TO GOD.

___RB 050 *Return To "First Love"*

(1) The example of the Church at Ephesus (Rev. 2:1-7). (2) The example of Mary Magdalene (Luke 7:36-47): First love is lavish, extravagant, personal, sacrificial, devotion without measure. The contrast of Simon the Pharisee. (3) The example of Mary Magdalene after the resurrection (John 20:1-18): First love is captivated by Christ, has eyes for Him only, nothing else on earth can satisfy it. (4) First love comes from an undivided heart which is captivated by Christ.

___RB 052 *God's Program For Deliverance*

God's deliverance program began in and through Jesus Christ. (1) Jesus was manifested to destroy the works of the devil (I John 3:8). (2) Jesus took from Satan the keys of hell and death. (Rev. 1:18) (3) Jesus spoiled principalities and powers (Col. 2:14-15). A discussion of the dangers of overemphasizing the demonic and why the devil wants us to do this. The difference between the works of the flesh and demons. The key is yielding to God and using your authority to resist the devil. Don't chase out the darkness, just bring in the light.

___054 *Thanking God For (In) All Things*

"The Lord knows how to deliver the godly out of temptations" (II Peter 2:9) and trials (Psalm 34:19). But we thank God "in" all things for several reasons: (1) Because all things - even tribulations - work together for good in our lives (Romans 8:28). (2) Trials (when embraced by faith) make us more like Jesus (Romans 8:29). We are to rejoice and be thankful, knowing this (James 1:2-4). (3) Trials move us closer to God and make us more effective witnesses. Discussion of how we close ourselves off from God's power in difficult situations if we do not thank Him in them. Pertinent illustrations from everyday life.

___RB 056 *The Rapture Of The Church*

A relating of several examples of angelic visitation to Christians with the message, "The Lord is coming again very soon." Also, several examples of dreams and visions about the Lord's coming for His people. These supernatural signs of His coming are being given to an increasing number of Christians. A discussion of the Rapture of the Church: I Thess. 4:13-18, I Cor. 15:51-57, Song of Solomon 2:8-14 and other passages. Also a discussion about how to prepare and be ready for the Lord's coming, including I John 3:2-3; II Peter 3:10-18.

____RB 058 *Why Some Christians Are Not Healed*

Healing and health are God's will for every Christian. They have been provided for us in Christ's atonement (I Peter 2:24). However, some Christians are not healed because blockages to God's blessing and healing power exist in certain areas of their lives. Discussion of certain blockages such as: (1) unforgiveness and roots of bitterness (2) lack of love (3) lack of faith (4) disobedience in giving tithes and offerings (5) improper care of the body (6) touching God's anointed (7) not discerning Christ's body...and so forth.

____RB 060 *Forgiveness-The Key to a Fuller Life*

A recounting of a four-hour conversation with Jesus on an airplane where much was revealed about the subject of forgiveness. What forgiveness is. The necessity of forgiveness. The relationship between healing, God's life and forgiveness. Discussion of Mt. 18:21-35, Eph. 4:42, Jas. 2:13, etc. The scope and inflexibility of Jesus' teaching on forgiveness. Forgiveness as release. HOW to forgive...especially in relationships. Many illustrations in everyday life. PRACTICAL, DYNAMIC AND NECESSARY IN EVERYDAY LIVING.

____RB 062 *The Ministry Of Angels*

References to angels far outnumber references to evil spirits in the Bible. God's emphasis is a healthy one. (1) A discussion of the purposes of angels in (A) praise and worship of God (B) protection (C) provision (D) punishment (E) delivering God's messages. (2) The relating of present day experiences with angels against the light of Biblical background. (SEE BOOKLET ON ANGELS).

____RB 064 *The Motivational Gifts*

(Introduction)

These gifts, seven in number, relate to HOW GOD FLOWS THROUGH YOU. (Romans 12:3-8). The seven different motivational gifts and their characteristics: (1) prophecy (2) serving (3) teaching (4) exhorting (5) giving (6) facilitating (organizing) (7) showing mercy. To be a fulfilled, effective, productive Christian, one needs to understand the working of these motivational-functional gifts in a practical way.

____RB 066 *Discovering God's Gifts Within Yourself*

A powerful message about how God directs us and uses us by moving us with compassion toward those people who have needs. Then He meets those needs by the flow of His Spirit and giftings through us. This is compared to Jesus being moved with compassion by the same Holy Spirit who moves us with compassion today. Jesus (1) saw a need (2) was often moved with compassion (by the Holy Spirit) (3) then spiritual gifts were manifested to meet that need. (Mark 1:40-45, Mark 6:32ff, Luke 7:11-18). Examples in different lives today.

_____RB 068 *Eight Biblical Ways To Receive Healing*

It's God's will to heal you. He has at least eight different "delivery systems" through which you can receive your healing. These are receiving healing through: (1) Gifts of healings and special anointings for healing miracles (2) The laying on of hands (3) Anointing with oil and the prayer of faith (4) Believing and speaking God's Word (5) The prayer of agreement (6) Believing you receive it when you pray (7) Partaking of the Lord's supper with faith (8) Using the name of Jesus against the enemy. Plus other important information regarding divine healing.

_____RB 070 *Drinking In The Holy Spirit*

The contrast between the influence of wine in the kingdom of darkness and its effects and the influence of the Holy Spirit in the kingdom of light (Ephesians 5:18-21) and His effects, such as: (1) worship and praise (2) giving thanks to God in every situation (3) fitting in with God's plans (4) giving of one's substance (5) relaxed and flexible living (6) boldness in witness (7) richness in fellowship. How the Holy Spirit produces *EVIDENCE.*

_____RB 072 *God, Our Supplier (Phil. 4:19)*

(1) God is our Source. (2) How to release God's resources in Christ through giving in faith. (3) God's riches in glory are IDEAS, knowledge and wisdom, which we follow by faith into greater spiritual and material prosperity. (4) How God showers down material supplies to us in the form of IDEAS which change lives and situations.

FAITH MESSAGES

_____RB 020 *The Growing Power Of Faith*

Mustard seed size faith will not produce one miracle. (1) It is faith that GROWS as a grain of mustard seed, ten or twelve foot high faith, the size of the mustard tree that works miracles. (2) The difference between unbelief, little faith and miracle working faith. (3) How faith grows depends on your hearing and obeying God's Word. Discussion of Luke 17:5-6, Mt. 17:14, 21, Mk. 4:30-32. (SEE BOOK BY SAME TITLE).

_____RB 022 *What Faith Is And Is Not*

The characteristics of faith: Natural and supernatural faith. (1) Faith is not sight (2) Faith is not hope (3) Faith is not mental assent (4) Faith is not presumption. Examples.

____RB 024 *The Divine Exchange*

(1) Jesus took the curse of the law (for our disobedience) upon Himself which included: spiritual death, physical sickness and disease and material poverty, (2) He gave us, in exchange, the reward for His obedience: eternal life, physical healing and health and material prosperity. (3) How God expects us to live in what He has provided.

____RB 026 *The Creative Power Of God's Word*

Creative Word of God is the Spirit empowered Word of God which (1) created and still dominates the universe today (2) produces faith in us (3) changes us (4) we can stop that creative power from working by doubt or unbelief.

____RB 028 *Speak The Word*

The importance of speaking the Word of God (Numbers 14:28, Mark 11:22-23, Proverbs 18:20-21). (1) How God's Words are like seeds and (2) How you reap a harvest of what you consistently say (Isaiah 57:19, Proverbs 6:2). (3) How God has told us to cling tenaciously to our profession (HOMOLOGIA) or saying the *SAME WORDS* God has said (Psalm 107:2.) A discussion of the principle of Romans 10:8-10.

____RB 030 *How To Increase Your Faith*

(1) The *planting* of faith (Ephesians 2:8, Rms. 10:17, Rms. 12:3) (2) The *pattern* of faith (Mark 5:25-29, I Samuel 17:40ff) (3) The *production* of your faith (Acts 11:13-14, Acts 14:7-10). How to increase your faith by *hearing, speaking,* and *acting* on the Word of God. (Included in book, *The Growing Power of Faith*).

CASSETTE SERIES
$5.00 PER CASSETTE
____RB 002-008 *How You Can Know God's Will*
(GUIDANCE) - 4 cassettes

PART I: God wants to guide...into blessing and fruitfulness. Prerequisites and misconceptions in guidance. Where God's will can be found. Progressive guidance, unconditional and conditional guidance. Direct and indirect guidance. The heart, the Word of God, the peace of God in guidance. *PART II:* Circumstances in guidance. Unconscious, providential guidance. Open doors and opportunities. Divine resistance and divine confirmation through circumstances. *PART III:* The inward witness, the voice of the human spirit, God's voice through the Holy Spirit in guidance. Also, godly counsel and prophecy in guidance. *PART IV:* More spectacular guidance through visions, dreams, prophecies, angelic visitations and the audible voice of God in guidance. The necessity to evaluate guidance.

___RB 010-012 *How To Test Christian Ministry & Guidance*

2 cassettes

This series includes: The *command* to "test all things", as well as the *process and results of testing*. The tests God has revealed must be applied as follows (1) Is it scriptural: sometimes not all black or white, but a question of mixture and balance. (2) Does it glorify Jesus? (3) Does it bear witness to your spirit? (4) Check the fruit of the ministry and the life. (5) Does it produce freedom or bondage? (6) If it is prophecy, does it come to pass? How these tests apply to judging personal prophecy, guidance, actions, etc., as well as Christian ministry. (SEE BOOK, "HOW TO TEST PROPHECY, PREACHING & GUIDANCE").

___RB 074-076 *How God Restores Human Personality*

2 cassettes

How God progressively rebuilds and restores the soul area (mind and emotions) by His Holy Spirit (Nehemiah means "consoler" or "comforter"). God gives us a picture of the process of recovery from points of bondage and captivity, of the rebuilding of the human personality by the Holy Spirit in the book of Nehemiah. This progressive recovery is a process of healing and refurbishing us as Christians which involves our co-operation and responsibility. Rich in practical truths.

___RB 078-079 *How To Meditate In God's Word*

079A   3 cassettes

(A) The command to meditate on God's Words. (B) What Christian meditation is. (C) The 7 steps God's Word takes in us as we meditate in it and His power is released:(1) INVESTIGATION (2) INCUBATION (3) ILLUMINATION (4) IMPARTATION (5) INSPIRATION (6) TRANSFORMATION and (7) MANIFESTATION.

___RB 080-090 *The Revelation Gifts Of the Spirit*

6 cassettes

WORD OF KNOWLEDGE

(A) How it operates (B) How it is used to: (1) reveal needs (2) expose corruption in the church (3) encourage believers (4) convince people of their need for Christ as Savior (5) provide needed information and help recover lost articles (6) protect and guide God's people (7) aid in effective prayer.

WORD OF WISDOM
(A) How it operates (B) How it is used to: (1) reveal God's purpose for a christian's life (2) to prepare for our wonderful future change in guidance (3) to provide assurance of coming deliverance in difficult times (4) to reveal special ministries (5) to reveal the right order and manner of divine worship (6) to reveal God's will in all his commands and ordinances.

DISCERNING OF SPIRITS
(A) How it operates (B) How it is used: (1) to help in delivering the afflicted and oppressed (2) to expose demonic activity and the enemy's servants (3) to help stop the devil's plans (4) to expose error and counterfeit manifestations by the enemy. What the discerning of the spirits is and is not. Discerning the similitude of God, the risen Christ, the Holy Spirit and also the human spirit in its good and evil tendencies.

____RB 092-096 *The Power Gifts of the Holy Spirit*
3 cassettes

THE GIFT OF FAITH
The definition of the gift, its operation and uses. The difference in saving faith and the gift of faith. Used to: (1) minister the baptism of the Spirit (2) raise the dead (3) cast out evil spirits (4) receive supernatural sustenance (5) pronounce blessings from God. This gift works in connection with the gift of working of miracles.

THE GIFT OF WORKING OF MIRACLES
What it is and how it operates. It is used: (1) to miraculously deliver God's people (Exodus 7-14). (2) to provide for those in want (I Kings 17:12-16) (3) to carry out divine judgment (Acts 5:1-5) (4) to confirm the preached Word (Acts 13:4-12) (5) to deliver from a dangerous situation (Acts 27) (6) to display God's power and magnificence.

THE GIFTS OF HEALINGS
What it is and how it operates. Used to: (1) heal the sick (2) discussion of the difference between faith healing and "grace-healing" (3) examples of present day healings.

2 NFCC IS A TOTAL LIVING CHRISTIAN CENTER

PURPOSES:
To provide an opportunity for Christian families to live, develop spiritually and help with Christian ministry in close proximity to Roxanne Brant Ministries and NFCC spiritual, educational and recreational activities which they support as members of the Church. (This especially provides retired and less mobile members of the NFCC Total Living Christian Center with opportunities to live economically (on low incomes) and yet near the spiritual, educational, recreational activities which are a necessary balance for their lives. These older members of Christ's Church will also be able to be involved in ministries of prayer and helps as their time, desires and energies allow.)

FACILITIES AND AREA
240 acres of beautiful, moss-laden oak forests and quiet, shaded pine glades interspersed with green fields provide a restful setting for living.

Different amounts of acreage have been alloted for mobile homes (48 half-acre tracts), the Headquarters-Church Complex (40 acres), homes (80 acres of 1 and 2 acre tracts) and a nature and agricultural area (60 acres). See the NFCC layout diagram above.

The N.F.C.C. Church provides enriching spiritual programs as well as exciting Christian educational programs for adults and children of all ages.

1 NFCC IS A RETREAT CENTER

PURPOSES:
To provide a place for ministers, congregations and individual Christians to meet for spiritual renewal and enrichment as well as for healing, equipping for Christian ministry and rest.

FACILITIES INCLUDE:
Furnished mobile units and rooms for visitors (in many nearby motels). Church sanctuary, multi-purpose conference, video and prayer rooms. Kitchen and dining areas, snack shop, swimming pool and picnic areas. Camp sites and hook-ups with toilet/shower and laundry facilities...all in a woodland setting.

Recreational areas and programs include much, from swimming, baseball, basketball, volleyball and ping pong to hiking and hayrides. Nearby, canoeing, skindiving and tubing on the Ichetucknee, Suwannee and Santa Fe Rivers as well as horseback riding provide for exciting activity.

3 NFCC IS THE CHURCH AND HEADQUARTERS COMPLEX OF

Roxanne Brant Ministries

Another name for NFCC is Roxanne Brant Ministries. The church and headquarters complex of Roxanne Brant Ministries are located in the center of the 240 acre platted property diagrammed above.

PURPOSE AND OUTREACHES:
Roxanne Brant Ministries has many outreaches. It holds **evangelistic / miracle crusades** throughout North America and other parts of the world. Through that outreach and its **publications outreach,** including books, tracts, leaflets and monthly newsletters, thousands of Christians have been strengthened and hundreds have found Christ. Over 1,000 ministers receive free Christian materials and encouragement through our **ministers outreach.** Through our **Prayer Corps outreach,** nearly 1,000 intercessors release God's blessings into areas of need. Local outreaches into prisons, to the unchurched, the needy and children tell and demonstrate God's love and good news of Christ.

COME AND VISIT US IN FLORIDA AT NORTHERN FLORIDA CHRISTIAN CENTER

NORTHERN FLORIDA CHRISTIAN CENTER is located on 240 acres of lovely country beauty. This Christian Total Living Center is nestled in the rolling hills of Northern Florida's lush green farm-ranch country. The **homes** here range from beautiful wood and brick homes to **mobile homes** in our 40 acre mobile home park.

NFCC is not only a Spirit-filled and Christ-exalting **Christian Total Living Center,** but it is also a **Church** and the **base of Roxanne Brant Ministries.** As such, so perfectly placed in nature's beautiful setting, the facilities are also used for seminars, conferences, retreats and camps. Here, hundreds of Christians come for rest and spiritual refreshment amidst the moss-laden oak forests and quiet, shaded pine glades.

We share good food, fun and fellowship in the beauty of God's creation.

NFCC exists for PEOPLE, - to bring them to Jesus Christ and to help them grow and become productive in and for Him. People from all parts of the United States have joined us here to grow and work for Jesus. They come from all walks of life: missionaries, ministers, builders, professional people, farmers... and so forth, working together in God's exciting service.

Our staff includes full time, part time and volunteer workers. In fact, volunteers are a large part of the Center's work force, doing office and maintenance helps, children's, youth and outreach ministries, errands, cooking and even cleaning. **WE NEED MORE VOLUNTEERS TO WORK FOR JESUS. IF YOU ARE INTERESTED, WRITE OR CALL LOUISE PAN AT (904) 935-0948.**